MACMILLAN

EMMA BY

MACMILLAN MASTER GUIDES

General Editor: James Gibson

Published:
JANE AUSTEN: **EMMA** Norman Page
ROBERT BOLT: **A MAN FOR ALL SEASONS** Leonard Smith
EMILY BRONTË: **WUTHERING HEIGHTS** Hilda D. Spear
GEOFFREY CHAUCER: **THE PROLOGUE TO THE CANTERBURY TALES** Nigel Thomas and Richard Swan
CHARLES DICKENS: **GREAT EXPECTATIONS** Dennis Butts
GEORGE ELIOT: **SILAS MARNER** Graham Handley
GEORGE ORWELL: **ANIMAL FARM** Jean Armstrong
WILLIAM SHAKESPEARE: **MACBETH** David Elloway
A MIDSUMMER NIGHT'S DREAM Kenneth Pickering
ROMEO AND JULIET Helen Morris

Forthcoming:
JANE AUSTEN: **MANSFIELD PARK** Richard Wirdnam
PRIDE AND PREJUDICE Raymond Wilson
CHARLES DICKENS: **HARD TIMES** Norman Page
GEORGE ELIOT: **MIDDLEMARCH** Graham Handley
T. S. ELIOT: **MURDER IN THE CATHEDRAL** Paul Lapworth
OLIVER GOLDSMITH: **SHE STOOPS TO CONQUER** Paul Ranger
THOMAS HARDY: **FAR FROM THE MADDING CROWD** Colin Temblett-Wood
TESS OF THE D'URBERVILLES James Gibson
CHRISTOPHER MARLOWE: **DR FAUSTUS** David Male
THE METAPHYSICAL POETS Joan van Emden
WILLIAM SHAKESPEARE: **HAMLET** Jean Brooks
TWELFTH NIGHT Edward Leeson
THE WINTER'S TALE Diana Devlin
GEORGE BERNARD SHAW: **ST JOAN** Leonee Ormond
R. B. SHERIDAN: **THE RIVALS** Jeremy Rowe

Also published by Macmillan

MACMILLAN MASTER SERIES

Mastering English Literature R. Gill
Mastering English Language S. H. Burton
Mastering English Grammar S. H. Burton

MACMILLAN MASTER GUIDES

EMMA

BY JANE AUSTEN

NORMAN PAGE

M
MACMILLAN

First edition 1985

Published by
MACMILLAN EDUCATION LTD
Houndmills, Basingstoke, Hampshire RG21 2XS
and London
Companies and representatives
throughout the world

Typeset by
TECSET, Sutton, Surrey

Printed in Hong Kong

British Library Cataloguing in Publication Data
Page, Norman
A Macmillan master guide to Emma.–
(Macmillan master guides)
1. Austen, Jane. Emma
I. Title
823′.7 PR4034.E53
ISBN 0-333-38005-3
ISBN 0-333-39303-1 (export)

CONTENTS

GENERAL EDITOR'S PREFACE

The aim of the Macmillan Master Guides is to help you to appreciate the book you are studying by providing information about it and by suggesting ways of reading and thinking about it which will lead to a fuller understanding. The section on the writer's life and background has been designed to illustrate those aspects of the writer's life which have influenced the work, and to place it in its personal and literary context. The summaries and critical commentary are of special importance in that each brief summary of the action is followed by an examination of the significant critical points. The space which might have been given to repetitive explanatory notes has been devoted to a detailed analysis of the kind of passage which might confront you in an examination. Literary criticism is concerned with both the broader aspects of the work being studied and with its detail. The ideas which meet us in reading a great work of literature, and their relevance to us today, are an essential part of our study, and our Guides look at the thought of their subject in some detail. But just as essential is the craft with which the writer has constructed his work of art, and this is considered under several technical headings – characterisation, language, style and stagecraft.

The authors of these Guides are all teachers and writers of wide experience, and they have chosen to write about books they admire and know well in the belief that they can communicate their admiration to you. But you yourself must read and know intimately the book you are studying. No one can do that for you. You should see this look as a lamppost. Use it to shed light, not to lean against. If you know your text and know what it is saying about life, and how it says it, then you will enjoy it, and there is no better way of passing an examination in literature.

JAMES GIBSON

ACKNOWLEDGEMENTS

Cover illustration: *A View of the Avon Gorge* by Francis Danby, courtesy of the City of Bristol Museum and Art Gallery and the Bridgeman Art Library.

1 JANE AUSTEN: LIFE AND BACKGROUND

Jane Austen was born on 16 December 1775 at Steventon, Hampshire, the seventh of the eight children of the Reverend George Austen and his wife Cassandra (née Leigh). This large family lived at the Rectory, in the village of Steventon, which is just off the road from Basingstoke to Andover; apart from the church, very little of the village as Jane Austen knew it now survives. In the pre-railway age, life in a country district would centre very much on the family and the village (just as it does in *Emma*); but with six brothers and a sister life can hardly have been dull for Jane. Family life was always important to her, and plays a prominent role in her novels, where she repeatedly explores the relationships of parents and children and of siblings. She was fortunate in being born to what Marghanita Laski describes as 'happy, talented parents and. . .a pleasant home', and she enjoyed particularly close relationships with her brother Henry, four years older than herself, and her sister Cassandra, two years older. Another of her brothers, Edward, had, like Frank Churchill in *Emma*, been adopted by wealthy relatives who were childless and was being brought up as their heir.

The Austens were comfortably off and life, though outwardly uneventful, must have been very pleasant. Middle-class life, especially rural life, in the southern counties of England is the favourite setting in Jane Austen's novels, which reflect the world she knew intimately from first-hand experience.

For a few years from the ages of six or seven to eleven or twelve Jane Austen was sent, with her sister Cassandra, to small boarding schools: first in Oxford, then in Southampton and finally in Reading. After that her education, like that of Emma Woodhouse, was acquired at home, but it seems to have been much more substantial than Emma's, for her father had a good library and the girls were allowed to read whatever they wished. To quote Marghanita Laski again:

> Since the popular picture of Jane Austen was formed in later Victorian times. . .it is important to remember that she was in fact a Georgian and brought up in the frank atmosphere of that enlightened age, an atmosphere in no way incompatible with the sincere if unostentatious Christianity of the Austen family.

Jane seems to have read widely if unsystematically, and her work contains allusions to a variety of authors, including poets and dramatists as well as novelists. The family were great novel-readers, and works of fiction were regularly read aloud in the family circle. Jane knew French and some Italian, played the piano and sang (like Jane Fairfax), did needlework and, as her letters later showed, was interested in clothes and the latest fashions in bonnets and gowns.

In such a busy, talented, bookish family, reading naturally stimulated writing, and Jane Austen's earliest surviving compositions date from the period 1787–93. These juvenile writings have been published and show a lively, high-spirited and fertile young author who instinctively turns to comedy and satire, many of these short pieces being parodies of the absurder elements in the fiction of the day. By the age of twenty or therabouts, she had written and read aloud to her family an episolary novel (written in the form of letters) called *Elinor and Marianne*. This was later extensively re-written and was published in 1811 as *Sense and Sensibility*. Soon afterwards she wrote another novel, *First Impressions*, which in turn, and much later, became *Pride and Prejudice*. Although, therefore, she published nothing until she was in her mid-thirties, her career as a serious author began early and was perseveringly followed.

Jane Austen's outer life was undramatic; she lived quietly with her family, never married and died fairly young, but there are a few landmarks that are worth drawing attention to. Although she remained unmarried she did not lack suitors and we know a little about four of them. When she was about twenty she met a handsome young Irishman called Tom Lefroy and there was at the very least a flirtation between them. In one of her letters she describes him as 'a very gentlemanlike, good-looking, pleasant young man'. But the dependence of marriage on money, so important in Jane Austen's novels, also applied to real life: neither she nor Tom had money, and he went back to Ireland. Soon afterwards a fellow of a Cambridge college called Samuel Blackall showed an interest in her, but she did not return it. The most important of the four relationships had a tragic outcome. In 1801, while on holiday in Devon, Jane met a young clergyman and the two of them fell in love; soon afterwards, however, he died. In the following year she seems to have received a proposal from a young man six years younger than herself; she accepted him one evening but then changed her mind the next day.

Her quiet life at home was often interrupted by visits to relatives and friends, and as her brothers grew up, followed various careers, married and had children of their own, she took a great interest in the expanding Austen clan and seems to have been a favourite aunt to her nieces and nephews. Her surviving letters, about 150 in number, give many glimpses of her daily life as well as an attractive impression of her vivacious, witty, often irreverent personality. The earliest letters date from 1796, and most of them are written to her sister Cassandra. It is necessary to say 'surviving letters' since Cassandra destroyed a large number of Jane's letters, including presumably the most intimate and revealing, after her sister's death; thus there are, for instance, no letters at all for a period of three and a half years after the tragic love affair referred to above.

Some of the letters show Jane Austen to have been very different from the prim spinster that she is sometimes thought of as having been. She was, for instance, very fond of dancing as well as of going to the theatre, and the Austen family sometimes organised their own private theatricals. Her familiarity with the drama had its effect on her novels, where the dialogue often has a crispness and economy that recall a well-written play.

We have only an approximate idea of Jane Austen's personal appearance. The only authentic portrait of her is a rather inexpert sketch by her sister Cassandra, now in the National Portrait Gallery in London. A number of verbal descriptions have also survived, some of them written much later. One depicts her as 'fair and handsome, slight and elegant, but with cheeks a little too full' (the full cheeks are evident in her sister's drawing); others describe Jane and Cassandra as 'perfect Beauties' and 'two of the prettiest girls in England'. The writer Miss Mitford recalled local gossip that Jane was 'the prettiest, silliest, most affected, husband-hunting butterfly' in her youth. One of the most detailed descriptions was given after her death by her niece Caroline, who states that 'hers was the first face that I can remember thinking pretty' and recalls her aunt's rather round face, dark brown hair curling naturally, good complexion and (like Emma) hazel eyes. Some of the accounts refer to her as slightly taller than average. Even if allowances are made for a degree of idealisation in the posthumous accounts, she seems to have been an attractive person always neat and even elegant in her appearance.

A turning point in Jane Austen's life occurred in 1800, when her father rather abruptly decided to retire and to move to Bath. Family tradition tells that when the news was given to Jane, she fainted; she had lived all her life in rural Hampshire, apparently had no wish to move to a busy town, and never seems to have been very happy in Bath, where she spent several years. After the death of her father at the beginning of 1805, the family income was greatly diminished, and after a short time Mrs Austen and her daughters moved first to Southampton and then in 1809 to the village of

Chawton, on the outskirts of Alton in Hampshire. Their house there, situated on the main road from London to Portsmouth, is small but pleasant and Jane Austen must have been gratified to return to her native Hampshire. The house is now open to the public.

Up to this time, although Jane Austen had been writing since childhood, she had published nothing. A novel of hers titled *Susan* had actually been bought by a London publisher in 1803, but for some reason he had never brought it out; later Jane Austen revised it and it was published after her death under the title *Northanger Abbey*. Once settled at Chawton Cottage, she seems to have applied herself to revising, and seeking publication for, some of her earlier work, as well as embarking on new enterprises. In 1809–10 she revised *Sense and Sensibility* and began the revision of *First Impressions*, which was later to appear as *Pride and Prejudice*. Early in 1811 she began *Mansfield Park* and at the end of the year *Sense and Sensibility* appeared. Like all Jane Austen's novels published in her lifetime, it was published anonymously, bearing the phrase 'By a Lady' on the title page (a common enough custom at that time).

Pride and Prejudice was published at the beginning of 1813 and *Mansfield Park*, completed that summer, appeared in the following year. Meanwhile, on 21 January 1814 (according to Cassandra Austen), Jane had begun *Emma*, the composition of which seems to have occupied her for just over a year. Though it has the date 1816 on the title page of the first edition, *Emma* was published in December 1815 in the conventional three-volume format; the title page states that it is 'By the author of "Pride and Prejudice", &c. &c.'.

Jane Austen's earlier novels had had a modest success, and there is evidence of her growing fame in the fact that *Emma* was dedicated, at his request, to the Prince Regent (later King George IV). She must have been gratified to learn that he kept a set of her books at each of the royal residences. Another sign of her success was the appearance at about this time of the first translations of her books. A French translation of *Sense and Sensibility* appeared in 1815, and versions of *Mansfield Park* and *Emma* (the latter under the title *La Nouvelle Emma, ou les Caractères Anglais du Siècle*) in 1816. There was also in 1816 an American edition of *Emma*.

Jane Austen was to write one more novel, *Persuasion*, published posthumously. It is striking evidence of her creative energies at this time that she seems to have begun it within a few months of completing, and well before the publication of, *Emma*. *Persuasion* was finished in August 1816, but by now Jane Austen was already in failing health. In May 1816 she had gone to Cheltenham with her sister, hoping that the medicinal waters at that spa might do her some good; but her illness was deep-seated and was to prove fatal. Its nature was not understood at the time, and her doctors were helpless; but we now know that she was suffering from Addison's disease, a wasting disease identified and named only in the mid-nineteenth century. One of the symptoms is a discoloration of the skin, and there may be some significance in the fact that the heroine of *Persuasion* is said to have lost her 'bloom' or youthful freshness of complexion.

She did not stop writing, and at the beginning of 1817 started a new novel, *Sanditon*, of which only a fragment was completed. She was now a dying woman, and in May 1817 moved to Winchester to be near a doctor who was treating her. Nursed devotedly by Cassandra she remained at the house in College Street where she had taken lodgings until the end and died in a bedroom there on 18 July at the age of forty-one. The house, which still stands and now bears a plaque over the door in memory of Jane Austen, is in the shadow of Winchester Cathedral, where she was buried and where her grave, with a touching inscription, may be seen. At the end of that year *Northanger Abbey* and *Persuasion* were published, together with a short biographical note by her brother Henry which names her as the author of her novels.

Students sometimes refer to Jane Austen as an eighteenth-century writer and sometimes as a Victorian writer. Neither statement is true. Admittedly she was born in the eighteenth century and more than half her short life was lived before 1800, but all her books were published in the nineteenth century. On the other hand, she died twenty years before Queen Victoria came to the throne, and indeed before Victoria was even born. She was in fact a Georgian writer: King George III, who had come to the throne fifteen years before her birth, was not succeeded by his son until three years after her death, though in his later years - the years during which her novels were published - he was incapacitated by mental illness and his son ruled in his stead with the title of Prince Regent. She may therefore be accurately described as a Regency writer.

Jane Austen lived through one of the most exciting periods of English history, when England was engaged in a life-and-death struggle with France and, at times, the threat of invasion (particularly to those who, like Jane Austen, lived near the south coast) seemed imminent. But one would never guess this from her books; nor did she intend that one should. *Emma* was published only six months after the Battle of Waterloo, but scarcely the faintest whisper of the great conflict with France is heard in the novel. This was not because she knew nothing or cared nothing about it: she had two brothers in the Navy and must have had some anxieties over their safety; moreover a member of the family had married a Frenchman who was sent to the guillotine. So that contemporary history, if it hardly touches her work, touched her private life and feelings. She was determined, however, to write only of those things that she thoroughly understood from first-hand experience; and clearly, for a woman in her situation, to write of war and battles could only have been a retailing of experience at second- or third-hand. On a smaller scale, it has been pointed out that, although male characters are important in her novels, she never shows men alone together – for the obvious and sufficient reason that she was in no position to know what they talked about, or what kind of language they used, on such occasions.

What Jane Austen does do is to give us, accurately and in detail, a picture of the life of the middle class, especially the rural middle class, around the turn of the century. (There are no references in *Emma* that enable us to assign the action to a particular year, but it is clearly a novel of contemporary life.) During her lifetime the Industrial Revolution got well under way and transformed life, especially urban life, in the north of England, but the southern counties were still relatively unaffected by change; and although there is a reference to the Churchills' great estate in Yorkshire, and a sense throughout that London is not far away (Frank Churchill rides there and back in a day), we may suppose Highbury to be in its essentials an eighteenth-century town and the Woodhouses to dwell in a gracious and spacious Georgian house.

Although life was physically restricted in many ways compared with modern times, there is a good deal of coming and going in *Emma*: Frank Churchill moves between his home and Highbury, Jane Fairfax arrives after the departure of the Campbells for Ireland, the John Knightleys visit Highbury from London and discuss taking a seaside holiday, Mr Knightley goes from Highbury to stay with them in London, as does Harriet. Those who are hard up, like the Bates, keep no carriage and rely on the generosity of others for transport when they do not walk, but when the better-off families go out on a formal occasion, or travel from place to place, they do so in considerable style. On the Christmas Eve visit to Randalls, the Woodhouses and Knightleys take two carriages for four people, requiring four horses and four servants; and when the John Knightleys come down from London they have two carriages for themselves and their servants.

Some of the characters enjoy a good deal of leisure: Mr Woodhouse has clearly never done a stroke of work in his life, and of course there can be no question of Emma, as an heiress, following any other career than marriage or staying at home to look after her father. But Jane Fairfax expects to be employed as a governess, and the novel also includes a lawyer, a doctor and a clergyman, not to mention Mr Knightley, who works hard at supervising the management of his estate.

Behaviour is to a large extent governed by conventions that are for the most part cheerfully accepted and observed: hence there is something very surprising and even shocking about the clandestine engagement of Frank Churchill and Jane Fairfax when it at last becomes known. An unmarried girl does not venture out alone, and it is interesting to see how Jane Austen contrives matters that Harriet should have to confront the gypsies without support (she has a companion who flees at the first sign of trouble). Nor could there by any question of a correspondence between a couple who are not yet engaged, and this makes Jane Fairfax's unexplained visits to the post office seem all the more ominous. Formality also extends to language, including the ways in which people address each other. Emma is 'Miss Woodhouse' even to people who, like Miss Bates, have known her all her life; and even after their marriage Emma will continue to call her husband 'Mr Knightley' rather than 'George'.

A small point of interest is that meal-times were different from the ones we are accustomed to. It is made clear in *Emma* that the Woodhouses eat dinner, their main meal of the day, at four o'clock, and take supper later in the evening. The period before dinner was referred to as the morning even if it was in what we should regard as the early afternoon.

Although Jane Austen's roots were in the eighteenth century, she was the contemporary of the great Romantic poets; and, even though *Emma* may be regarded as an anti-romantic novel, it contains some signs of the new sensibility. The visit to Box Hill, for instance, is evidence of the taste for 'wild' landscape that had fairly recently developed. But the main thrust of the novel is, of course, against romanticism: Emma's follies are a direct result of an excess of imagination that is allowed to go uncontrolled. There is some pleasant satire against romantic folly when Mrs Elton proposes that, on the visit to Donwell Abbey to pick strawberries, they should picnic like gypsies; Mr Knightley, who stands for eighteenth-century common sense and distrust of affectation, insists that food be taken indoors sitting round a table.

A word may be added on the relative value of money in the period. To gain some idea of present-day values, figures would need to be multiplied ten or twenty times at least; hence Emma's fortune of thirty thousand pounds is a very large one, and even Miss Hawkins brings Mr Elton enough ('so many thousands as would always be called ten') to satisfy his avarice.

2 SUMMARIES AND CRITICAL COMMENTARY

2.1 INTRODUCTION

Each of the fifty-five chapters of *Emma* is examined below from two points of view:

(1) the content of the chapter (i.e. a brief summary of the main incidents it contains and its contribution to the development of the action)
(2) points of interest in relation to criticism and interpretation (the most important of these are discussed more thoroughly in Chapters 3 and 4).

Note When *Emma* was originally published in three volumes, each volume numbered the chapters from 1 onwards: the first volume contained eighteen chapters, the second also eighteen, and the final volume contained nineteen. Some modern editions retain this numbering, but others number the chapters straight through from 1 to 55. For ease of reference, both systems of numbering are used below, the indication in parenthesis referring to the original volume and chapter numbers: thus 20 (II, 2) means that the chapter in question was the second in the second volume.

2.2 CHAPTER SUMMARIES AND COMMENTARY

Chapter 1 (I, 1)

The Woodhouse family and other major characters are introduced. The first to be mentioned is the heroine, Emma Woodhouse, 'nearly twenty-one years' old and the younger daughter of Mr Woodhouse. Emma's mother has died in her early childhood, and for sixteen years Miss Taylor has been her governess, friend and mother-substitute; shortly before the action of the novel begins, however, Miss Taylor has married Mr Weston, a widower. Mr Woodhouse, Emma's father, is a fairly elderly man who married rather late in life, and has been 'a true valetudinarian all his life' (that is, he is excessively concerned about his health and about the illnesses, real or imaginary, of himself and others); he is a wealthy man who lives on his inheritance and is the leading citizen of Highbury, the small town where the action takes place, though he plays no part in local affairs and rarely ventures from his own home. Emma's sister is married and lives in London with her husband and children.

Apart from the Woodhouse family, we meet Mr Knightley, a man in his late thirties who is a close friend of theirs and is related to them by marriage, being the elder brother of Emma's sister's husband. Mr Knightley is a bachelor, as is Mr Elton, a clergyman of 'six or seven-and-twenty'.

In this chapter Mr Woodhouse, who dislikes change of any kind, expresses his regret that Mrs Weston has married and left them; Emma claims the credit for bringing about the marriage and announces her intention of doing the same for Mr Elton, upon which Mr Knightley advises her not to interfere in other people's lives.

Note that Jane Austen sketches in the small town that is to be the setting for her story: Highbury is sixteen miles from London (we learn later that it is in Surrey), and is 'a large and populous village almost amounting to a town'. Three of the largest houses are named: the Woodhouses live at Hartfield, the Westons at Randalls and Mr Knightley at Donwell Abbey.

Two important themes are touched on: that of marriage (the matrimonial status of each of the characters is clearly indicated, and there are no fewer than three unmarried and eligible persons among them), and that of Emma's fondness for arranging people's lives – a tendency that Mr Knightley is quite prepared to try to check. Since Emma's idea of settling her friends' futures takes the form of finding them wives or husbands, the two themes are linked.

Chapter 2 (I, 2)

Another major character – and another eligible bachelor – is introduced: Frank Churchill is the son of Mr Weston by his first marriage to a Miss Churchill, daughter of 'a great Yorkshire family' who have disowned her for marrying beneath her. After her death, however, the Churchills, who are childless, have taken care of the boy and have changed his name from Weston to Churchill. Mr Weston sees his son 'every year in London', but although Frank is often discussed in Highbury he has never been seen there. The chapter also mentions two Highbury families of lesser importance, the Perrys and the Bates. Mr Perry is an 'apothecary' or physician (doctors had a fairly humble social status at this time); the Bates are more fully described in the next chapter.

The main purpose of the chapter is to arouse curiosity with regard to Frank Churchill and to prepare the ground for his eventual, long-anticipated arrival in Highbury. Since he has been virtually adopted by a wealthy family, it may cross the reader's mind that he would make a very suitable husband for Emma (and Jane Austen no doubt intended that this possibility should be entertained). The history of Frank's parents, and specifically the disowning of his mother for making an unequal match, raise the issue of the relationship of marriage to money and property in English middle- and upper-class society - a recurring theme in this novel and in Jane Austen's work as a whole.

Chapter 3 (I, 3)

Further characters are introduced. Mrs Bates is 'the widow of a former vicar of Highbury'; she is an old lady in impoverished circumstances who lives with her middle-aged spinster daughter. Together with Mrs Goddard, who keeps a small school, the Bates visit the Woodhouses one evening, Mrs Goddard bringing with her one of her pupils, the seventeen-year-old Harriet Smith. Harriet is very pretty, with blue eyes and fair hair, and is 'the natural daughter of somebody' (that is, the illegitimate daughter of a man who, though he maintains her, has not disclosed his identity). Emma resolves to take Harriet under her wing and decides that she has been mixing in society unworthy of her (she has been befriended by the Martin family of Abbey-Mill Farm, who are tenant-farmers on Mr Knightley's estate).

In this chapter Jane Austen uses her favourite device of a social occasion - here the informal and small-scale one of an evening visit - to bring together a group of characters. Emma's romantic temperament can be detected in her feelings towards Harriet: because the latter's parentage is unknown, Emma assumes that she must be the daughter of a man of high social position. Her readiness to take charge of other people's lives is seen in her resolve to patronise Harriet, and her sense of her own social importance is seen both in her attitude to Harriet (who, even if she becomes Miss Woodhouse's friend, will clearly be her inferior) and in her attitude to the Martins, who are perfectly respectable and worthy people.

Chapter 4 (I, 4)

Harriet becomes a frequent visitor to Hartfield. Emma meets Robert Martin, the young farmer who is in love with Harriet, and decides that he is not a gentleman and is unworthy of her friend. She decides to make a match between Harriet and Mr Elton, the bachelor-vicar.

Again Emma's romantic impulsiveness and her social snobbery - both of which, combined with her fondness for arranging other people's lives, may have potentially disastrous results - are stressed. It is clear that Harriet, who is submissive and not very bright, satisfies Emma's taste for playing Lady Bountiful, as well as helping to fill the gap left in her life by the marriage of her former companion, Miss Taylor.

Chapter 5 (I, 5)

This chapter is devoted to a discussion between Mrs Weston and Mr Knightley on the subject of Emma. Mr Knightley tells Mrs Weston that the friendship with Harriet is bad for Emma, since it gives her too great a sense of her own virtues and importance.

The significant point here is the gradual emergence of Mr Knightley's relationship with Emma: he has known her all her life, is very fond of her, but is far from blind to her imperfections, which he is quite prepared to point out to others and to Emma herself. He is considerably older than Emma but much younger than her father, and thus occupies an elder-brotherly or quasi-tutorial position which is to be very important as the novel develops.

Chapter 6 (I, 6)

This takes up where Chapter 4 left off, with Emma doing what she can to foster the relationship between Harriet and Mr Elton. Mr Elton encourages Emma to draw a portrait of Harriet.

This incident provides a good example of the use of ambiguity and misinterpretation in the novel, especially in relation to Emma's perception of other people's true feelings. She jumps to the conclusion (because it is what she wants to believe) that Mr Elton is keen to have a picture of Harriet and that this is evidence of his feelings for her; it never occurs to Emma that Mr Elton may be more interested in the artist than in the subject, and that his desire for a picture may be a piece of flattery aimed at Emma herself (whose artistic abilities, it seems, are of a very limited kind). A close reading of this scene shows that Emma continually attaches one meaning to a speech or an action where it would be perfectly possible to attach another, quite different meaning; she thus finds her own desires fulfilled and her own suspicions confirmed, instead of contemplating the possibility that she might be wrong. Note how Jane Austen's method in this chapter combines narrative, dialogue, comment by the author or narrator, and a rendering of Emma's own unspoken thoughts.

Chapter 7 (I, 7)

Harriet now receives a letter from Robert Martin containing a proposal of marriage. Emma persuades her to refuse him, and encourages her to believe that Mr Elton loves her.

Emma's interference in her friend's life now takes a more dramatic turn: at Emma's instigation, Harriet turns down a man who would seem to be a highly suitable match for her in favour of a man of a higher social class whose interest in Harriet is no more than a supposition of Emma's.

Chapter 8 (I, 8)

Emma and Mr Knightley discuss Harriet (note that the ground for this scene has been prepared in Chapter 5 as well as in Chapters 6 and 7). When Knightley learns that Harriet has turned down Robert Martin, he is angry with Emma, accuses her of interference, and insists that Martin would be more than worthy of Harriet. He also tells her that Elton is not at all the kind of man to marry a girl such as Harriet, who is of obscure birth and has no dowry.

Knightley's role as the voice of realism and mature common sense, in contrast to Emma's romantic daydreams, is very striking here. He has a clear sense of Harriet's social position, Martin's merits, and Elton's ambition and self-seeking; he attempts, as so often, to bring Emma to her senses, but her self-confidence and vanity are too strong for her to admit herself to be in error.

Chapter 9 (I, 9)

Harriet makes a collection of riddles (a fair index of her intellectual limitations, and a wry comment by Jane Austen on what was considered to be a suitable occupation for a young lady). Elton contributes some, one of which is quoted (it has been suggested that the answer, which Jane Austen leaves to the reader to guess, is 'woman', i.e. woe-man), and composes one specially for the purpose. News arrives that Mr John Knightley, Isabella (Emma's sister), and their five children are to visit Hartfield for a week at Christmas.

The point about a riddle or charade is that it constitutes a puzzle to which a right or wrong answer can be given; it thus neatly represents the larger dramatic situation in which Emma, Harriet and Elton are involved, which is itself fraught with ambiguity and the possibility of misinterpretation. The situation here is to be paralleled in a later chapter, where Frank Churchill and Jane Fairfax play a different wordgame with similarly symbolic overtones. As in Chapter 6, ambiguous behaviour, and consequent misunderstandings, abound: for example, Mr Elton's confusion at the end of the chapter, when he learns that his riddle has been copied by Emma into Harriet's collection, is plainly capable of two interpretations - either he is flattered by Emma's copying it out, or Harriet's admiration for it is what excites him. Emma, of course, opts for the second alternative and never considers the first; but there is no objective evidence to suggest that she is necessarily right. Jane Austen carefully leaves the options open (e.g. Elton 'glanced at Emma and at Harriet') so that the reader either shares Emma's error or, at best, is left in suspense as to the true situation.

Chapter 10 (I, 10)

While out walking, Emma and Harriet discuss marriage. Emma tells her friend that she herself has 'none of the usual inducements of women to marry' - that is, the desire for social position and economic security. It becomes clear that she has never been in love. They meet Mr Elton by chance, and Emma contrives that they are invited into his house. He has an opportunity to propose to Harriet, but to Emma's surprise fails to take advantage of it.

Emma's lack of interest in marriage reflects her immaturity and absence of self-knowledge, and with hindsight can be seen to be unconsciously ironic, since her development in the novel is towards the maturity that makes her ready for acknowledged love and marriage. Her attempt to manipulate other people meets a check when Mr Elton fails to propose to Harriet, as Emma confidently expected him to do; but this is not enough to cause her to consider the possibility that she may be wrong and to revise her view of his attitude to Harriet and herself.

Chapter 11 (I, 11)

The John Knightleys arrive and are described. Frank Churchill is mentioned again, and his age is given as 23.

The John Knightleys' Christmas visit is one of numerous references to the time of year throughout the novel, which is constructed with a clear chronology. The action has begun, as R. W. Chapman points out, 'at or after the end of September', there are references to October and November in the opening chapter, and the incident in Chapter 10 takes place in mid-December. As later references will show, the entire action of the novel occupies about a year.

Chapter 12 (I, 12)

Mr Knightley joins the Woodhouses and their visitors for dinner. He and Emma engage in conversation, while Mr Woodhouse and his elder daughter discuss their favourite topic of doctors and ailments. There is a reference to Jane Fairfax, a niece of Miss Bates who is 'exactly Emma.s age' and is a governess with a family named Campbell.

The character-contrast between the two sisters, Emma and Isabella, is a marked one: Isabella, with her petty anxieties, is very much her father's daughter, while Emma, more intelligent and vivacious, presumably takes after her dead mother. (The contrasts within a family, and the effects of heredity, are a never-failing source of interest for Jane Austen.) Emma is seen here in an attractive light: her genuine concern for her father is shown by the way in which she skilfully steers the conversation away from topics that might upset him, and by her interventions in the role of peacemaker. Jane Fairfax, who is later to emerge as a major character, is introduced in a way that suggests that she is to be compared and contrasted with Emma: Jane is of the same age but occupies a very different social position.

Chapter 13 (I, 13)

On Christmas Eve, the Woodhouses and the John Knightleys are to dine at Randalls, the home of the Westons. Harriet and Mr Elton have also been invited; Harriet, however, is suffering from a sore throat and is 'very feverish', so is unable to be present. Mr Elton expresses great concern at Harriet's condition, but to Emma's surprise he indicates that he has every intention of turning up himself. In conversation, John Knightley suggests to Emma that she is the object of Mr Elton's interest, but she dismisses the notion. There is a turn for the worse in the weather, and it begins to snow, but this does not dissuade the guests from venturing out. In the carriage on the way to Randalls, Mr Elton is in high spirits - a further source of surprise to Emma (but perhaps not, by this stage, to the reader).

Once again, Emma's wilful refusal to abandon her own preconceived ideas in the face of the evidence can be seen. There is another example of ambiguity in Mr Elton's concern over Harriet's state of health: is he thinking of Harriet herself, or of the possibility that Emma may have caught the infection? She is puzzled when, instead of staying at home like a lover disappointed of seeing his beloved, he turns up in a state of cheerfulness; but she fails to draw any conclusions from this. When John Knightley directly suggests, on the basis of his own objective observation of the situation, that Elton's interest is in Emma herself, she still refuses to revise her ideas, since this would involve admitting that she has been wrong.

Chapter 14 (I, 14)

This continues the action initiated in the previous chapter. During dinner Mr Elton is assiduous in his attentions to Emma. Mr Weston mentions that he has received a letter from Frank Churchill, who is to visit his father and stepmother 'within a fortnight'. But it emerges that Mrs Churchill is a selfish and demanding woman, subject to sudden changes of mood, and the visit may well be cancelled at the last moment on account of some whim of hers. It remains unclear, however, whether Frank has been genuinely unable to come or has simply not troubled to make the required effort. Emma has never seen Frank, but the reader learns that she has 'frequently thought. . .that if she *were* to marry, he was the very person to suit her in age, character and condition' (condition here meaning social status).

Again, a social occasion, this time a dinner-party, enables Jane Austen to group her characters and develop the relationships between them. She arranges matters so that Harriet is not present, with the result that Elton's attitude towards Emma becomes less ambiguous (though still not perceived by Emma herself). The reader's curiosity concerning Frank Churchill is stimulated: Frank was mentioned in the second chapter of the novel, but has still not been seen. There is some ambiguity about his behaviour - is he really unable to pay a visit that is of some importance, since he has not yet met his new stepmother, or is he simply selfish and self-indulgent, and using Mrs Churchill's tyrannical behaviour as a convenient excuse? The reader may begin to suspect that his Christian name is ironically intended and that frankness is not one of his qualities.

Chapter 15 (I, 15)

The same scene is continued. As the party take tea in the drawing-room, Emma is greatly surprised and offended by the pertinacity of Mr Elton's attentions, and gives him a look of strong displeasure. It is now snowing heavily, 'with a strong drifting wind', and Mr Woodhouse is filled with consternation. They resolve to set out for home at once, and in the ensuing confusion Emma finds herself alone in the second carriage with Mr Elton, who loses no time in making an ardent proposal of marriage. When she tells him that she has believed his interest to have been in Harriet Smith, he replies that he has no interest at all in Harriet. Emma denies that she herself has given him any encouragement and makes it clear that she has no intention of accepting him; he is 'too angry to say another word'.

The scene in the carriage, a good example of 'reversal', forms the climax of the first phase of the novel and of the first instalment of Emma's efforts to usurp the role of Providence. She now is forced to recognise that all her suppositions up to this point concerning Elton and Harriet have been quite incorrect, and there are obvious implications for the immediate future (she will have to undeceive Harriet and to live with the awkward situation now existing between herself and Elton). We may again observe the skill with which Jane Austen contrives that Emma and Elton may be alone for long enough for him to make his proposal and to receive an answer: in normal circumstances, given the social conventions of the time, the two of them them would be unlikely ever to be left alone. Jane Austen also extracts comic effect from the haste and effusiveness of the proposal (Elton knows that he only has a few minutes) in the confined space of the carriage.

Chapter 16 (I, 16)

The first part of the chapter provides an insight into Emma's private thoughts and emotions: at home and alone at bedtime on the same evening as the incident in the previous chapter, she is full of shame and misery at having persuaded Harriet that Elton loved her. She realises that on various occasions, such as the episodes of the picture and the riddles, she has misinterpreted the evidence; she also admits to herself that the Knightley brothers had both separately been right in giving her hints of Mr Elton's true intentions. For the next few days she is housebound by the heavy snowfall, and thus is spared seeing either Harriet or Elton.

Emma's reactions to the new situation indicate her fundamental honesty and decency: she is genuinely upset at the prospect of Harriet's unhappiness, and is ready to recognise her own errors and obstinate refusal to see the truth. At the same time, none of this is likely to cure her tendency towards a romantic reshaping of reality, and there is no guarantee that she will not make the same mistakes again. Technically, the chapter is a good example of Jane Austen's ability - very exceptional in the fiction of her time - to give an insight into the inner life of her protagonist.

Chapter 17 (I, 17)

A short chapter in which the John Knightleys leave Hartfield to return to London; Mr Elton sends a message to say that he is leaving Highbury to spend a few weeks with friends in Bath; and Emma tells Harriet that Mr Elton has no interest in her.

Elton's departure concludes this first phase of Emma's follies and misapprehensions, and leaves the way open for the appearance within a few chapters of another young and eligible bachelor as a fresh source of romantic interest.

Chapter 18 (I, 18)

This chapter concludes the first volume of *Emma* in the original three-volume format. Frank Churchill cancels the visit promised in Chapter 13. Mr Knightley suggests to Emma that Frank is guilty of a lack of consideration towards his father, and remarks that 'I dare say he might come if he would', but Emma defends Frank.

Once more the reader's curiosity in Frank Churchill is whetted, and once more we find Emma making judgements without sufficient evidence, since she has no real grounds for defending Frank except a romantic interest in him. This long conversation on the morality of Frank's behaviour shows Mr Knightley taking up a firm position and stating it with conviction, while Emma fails to see the justice of his views. We may also suspect that Emma, consciously or otherwise, is coming to regard Frank as a potential replacement for Mr Elton: she declares that when he does eventually come he will be 'a treasure at Highbury'. The chapter thus acts as a bridge between the first two volumes and points forward to Emma's involvement with Frank in the coming chapters.

Chapter 19 (II, 1)

During a morning walk, Emma and Harriet pay a call on Miss Bates and her mother at their modest home (they have rooms in someone else's house). The Bates have just received a letter from Jane Fairfax, announcing that she will be arriving the following week: she has been unwell, and is coming home to recuperate. The visit is made possible by the departure of her employers, the Campbells, for Ireland, where they have gone to stay with a recently married daughter (Mrs Dixon). It emerges that Jane has acted as chaperone during the Dixons' courtship, and therefore is acquainted with Mr Dixon. Miss Bates' artless references to him as 'a most amiable, charming young man', together with a chance allusion to Jane's 'longing to go to Ireland', excite Emma's suspicions.

Jane Fairfax, like Frank Churchill, has been often referred to in the first volume of the novel but has not yet been seen. This chapter prepares the reader for her arrival and shows that Emma has not really learned from her recent painful experience: she immediately begins to imagine a romantic triangular situation in which Jane Fairfax has fallen in love with Mr Dixon and is heartbroken at his marriage to Miss Campbell.

We have in this chapter one more example of the importance of letters in Jane Austen's novels (compare Frank Churchill's earlier letters to his father, and note that there are several parallels between Frank and Jane in the way in which they are presented). In an age that lacked the telephone and in which travel was often expensive, slow and uncomfortable, letters played an important part in maintaining familial and social links in Jane Austen's period and in her own life.

Chapter 20 (II, 2)

More information is given concerning Jane Fairfax, 'an orphan, the only child of Mrs. Bates's youngest daughter', and hence the neice of Miss Bates, who is devoted to her. Orphaned at the age of three, she has spent long periods at the home of Colonel Campbell as companion for his own daughter, an only child; but now that Miss Campbell is married, she no longer has a function there and is shortly to take up the profession of governess for which she has been educated (she has resolved to take a position of this kind on reaching the age of twenty-one). Jane has not been in Highbury for two years. For reasons that are not very clear, even to herself, Emma does not much like Jane; but on meeting her again she is impressed by her beauty and refinement. It emerges that Jane has met Frank Churchill at the fashionable seaside resort of Weymouth, but she speaks of him without enthusiasm.

Jane Fairfax's role in the novel as a counterpart and foil to Emma now begins to become more obvious, and we may surmise that Emma sees in her, notwithstanding her greatly inferior social position, a potential threat to her own hitherto unrivalled supremacy in the small society of Highbury (Jane's beauty and elegance are stressed). As usual, it is Mr Knightley who sees the situation more clearly than anyone else, and who does not hesitate to try to make Emma see it too: 'Why she did not like Jane Fairfax might be a difficult question to answer; Mr Knightley had once told her it was because she saw in her the really accomplished young woman, which she wanted to be thought herself. . .'.

The final paragraph of the chapter, though unemphatic in tone, is of great importance. Emma finds in Jane the quality of 'reserve' - that is, the opposite of frankness - and the subject on which she is notably reserved is Frank Churchill. However, Emma, whose suspicions of Jane's feelings towards Mr Dixon continue, is not alerted by Jane's behaviour: ironically enough, Emma, who is eagerly pursuing a false trail, fails to recognise the clues to the real situation. (To be fair to Emma, however, these clues are very unobtrusively presented and are likely to be missed by the reader on a first reading.)

Chapter 21 (II, 3)

Emma, Mr Knightley and Mr Woodhouse discuss Jane Fairfax. Miss Bates and Jane arrive with the news that Mr Elton is to be married to a Miss Hawkins, whom he has met in Bath: since he has been gone from Highbury 'only four weeks', it is evidently a whirlwind romance. Later Harriet also arrives at Hartfield, having heard the news of Mr Elton's engagement.

The chapter recalls to our attention Mr Elton, who has disappeared only temporarily from the action of the novel, and promises a new character, Mrs Elton.

Chapter 22 (II, 4)

Mr Elton returns briefly to Highbury but soon sets off for Bath again for his wedding. It is learned that Miss Hawkins is the daughter of a Bristol tradesman and has a dowry of about ten thousand pounds.

Mr Elton's mercenary motives are now clearly exposed: having been turned down by an heiress, he has quickly made a match that, though inferior from the social as well as the financial point of view, is still satisfactory. Since Miss Hawkins' money comes from 'trade' rather than from land, and since she comes from the bustling commercial centre of Bristol, the question arises how she will fit into the small, class-conscious society of Highbury in rural Surrey.

Chapter 23 (II, 5)

Though still preoccupied by thoughts of Mr Elton, Harriet calls on the Martins. The Westons tell Emma that Frank Churchill will arrive the next day for a fortnight's visit. When Emma meets Frank on the next day she finds him 'a *very* good looking young man' and decides she will like him. Frank mentions that he knows Jane Fairfax and will pay a courtesy call on the Bates.

Emma's impulsiveness appears once again in her instant verdict in favour of Frank Churchill: influenced by his good looks, she knows very little of his true character. From the reader's point of view, Frank would seem to be a highly eligible match for Emma. Frank's intention of visiting the Bates almost immediately upon his arrival in Highbury provides a clue to the discerning reader, who may also be struck by the fact that he pays his long-deferred visit to Highbury immediately after Jane's arrival there.

Chapter 24 (II, 6)

The next day, having paid his visit to the Bates, Frank speaks critically to Emma and Mrs Weston of Jane Fairfax's appearance. When Emma asks if he has seen much of Jane at Weymouth, he first changes the subject then tries to avoid a direct answer to the question. He and Emma discuss Jane's character and agree in condemning her 'reserve'. When Frank declares that 'One cannot love a reserved person', Emma replies, with a relevance to the situation of which she is quite unaware, 'Not till the reserve ceases towards oneself, and then the attraction may be the greater'.

Frank Churchill's true relationship with Jane Fairfax, which only emerges towards the end of the novel, places both of them in a false position and is responsible for many ironies that become apparent only on a second reading. Frank tries to avoid telling direct lies; at the same time he is undoubtedly guilty of deceit, and he treats Emma badly in throwing dust in her eyes by joining with her in criticising Jane Fairfax; we may assume that he and Jane, in their moments of privacy, enjoy the joke of Emma's ready gullibility.

Chapter 25 (II, 7)

Frank goes to London, a distance of sixteen miles each way, ostensibly to have his hair cut - a piece of behaviour that looks like vanity. Despite this, the general verdict in Highbury is that he is a fine young man. Mr Knightley, however, dissents from this view and finds him 'a trifling, silly fellow'. The Coles, a Highbury family who have become prosperous and are socially ambitious, are to give a dinner party to which Emma, the Westons and Mr Knightley are invited.

The perceptive reader may well ask himself whether Frank's haircut is not merely an excuse and whether he has a different object in his visit to London. Mr Knightley's judgement of him is notably independent and forthright - and, as it subsequently turns out, not far from the truth. The ground is laid for another formal social occasion that will bring together a group of characters.

Chapter 26 (II, 8)

This important chapter is devoted to an account of the dinner party given by the Coles. It emerges that Jane Fairfax has received the surprise gift of a fine piano from an unknown donor, and there is speculation whether it has come from Colonel Campbell or from Mr Dixon. Frank Churchill pays particular attention to Emma and again criticises Jane Fairfax's appearance;

later he dances with Emma and tells her that he is glad to have escaped dancing with Jane. It emerges that Jane and her aunt have been brought to the Coles' house, and are to be taken home again, by Mr Knightley's carriage (naturally the Bates are much too poor to keep their own carriage), and Mrs Weston suspects that he may have a romantic interest in Jane and suggests that he may have sent the piano - ideas that Emma strongly opposes, with various reasons in support of her opinion. Mr Knightley shows no enthusiasm for Jane's singing.

The occasion is a typical middle-class evening party of the period, with conversation, dancing, and entertainment provided by such young ladies as can be prevailed upon to show off their accomplishments. Jane's piano is an object of mystery and stimulates a curiosity that is not to be satisfied until much later; it is also an example of the ambiguity so common in this novel, since the various donors who are proposed would all have their own reasons for making such a gift in such a way. (Note that Jane Austen makes relatively little use of physical objects, and that when they are used they often have a significant or symbolic function.) Another example of ambiguity is the pointed attentions that Frank pays to Emma: are they evidence of a genuine interest in Emma, or a smokescreen to conceal his true interest? His criticisms of Jane Fairfax seem somewhat excessive and over-insistent and may lead us to suspect that they, too, are not quite what they seem. A point of considerable psychological interest is Emma's strong opposition to the idea that Mr Knightley might be attracted to Jane Fairfax: why does she react so decidedly to this suggestion? We may suspect that, although she does not consciously realise it, she has taken it for granted that she herself stands first in Mr Knightley's good opinion, and she is unable to tolerate the notion of Jane as a rival.

Chapter 27 (II, 9)

While shopping in Highbury with Harriet, Emma happens to meet Mrs Weston and Frank Churchill, and they all visit the Bates' home to hear Jane's new piano.

Chapter 28 (II, 10)

As Jane plays to them, Frank refers to Colonel Campbell as the donor of the piano. Mr Knightley passes by and enquires after Jane; he is invited in, and it emerges in conversation that he has sent a gift of apples to Miss Bates.

The reason for Frank's reference to Colonel Campbell becomes apparent only much later in the novel: it is a private joke between Jane and himself at the expense of Emma. Mr Knightley's enquiry concerning Jane, and his gift of apples, seem to go some way towards confirming Mrs Weston's supposition that he has a romantic interest in Jane, and it may be that Jane Austen is here trying to send the reader off on a false scent. With hindsight, on the other hand, we can see that the modest gift of apples is a much more reasonable one, and more thoroughly in character for Mr Knightley, than the secret gift of a piano with which he has been credited by Mrs Weston. Here as elsewhere, Jane Austen plays strictly fair: nobody acts out of character, and the confusions and misunderstandings arise only because of the human tendency to jump to conclusions without sufficient evidence – to be guided by romantic impulse rather than reason. Mrs Weston's speculations suggest that she is slightly tarred with this brush, and since she has been responsible for Emma's education we may suppose that she is partly responsible for this tendency in Emma, or at least for leaving it unchecked.

Chapter 29 (II, 11)

Following the success of the dancing at the Coles' evening party in Chapter 26, a ball is planned, to take place at the Crown Inn, in spite of Mr Woodhouse's anxious fears about the risk to the health of those involved.

Chapter 30 (II, 12)

The ball planned in the previous chapter is cancelled, since Frank Churchill has been summoned to return home by the Churchills and his stay in Highbury is thus abruptly terminated. He pays a farewell visit to Emma and mentions to her that he has called on the Bates. He appears to be on the brink of making a confession, and Emma is convinced that he is in love with her, but he departs without any declaration.

By this point Emma is again involved in a tissue of self-delusion. The situation is the reverse of that relating to Mr Elton: this time Emma believes herself to be the true object of attention, but the fact is that Frank is merely using his flirtation with Emma somewhat heartlessly, or at least thoughtlessly, as a cloak for his clandestine relationship with Jane Fairfax. The situation is also more complex than the one in the earlier part of the book, in that there is also the question of who is attracted to Jane. Significantly, too, Emma's own feelings are, at least potentially, more fully engaged than in her schemings on behalf of Harriet. This second phase of Emma's comedy of errors is, therefore, no mere carbon copy of the first. Note how scrupulously Jane Austen provides the reader with the evidence necessary to form a correct judgment of what is going on: Frank's visit to the Bates is mentioned, and though this appears to be of minor importance in relation to his farewell to Emma, it is actually from his point of view of far greater importance.

Chapter 31 (II, 13)

In Frank's absence, Emma fancies herself mildly in love with him and believes him to be very much in love with her. Since she does not intend to marry, she will refuse him if he makes an offer. She decides to try to make a match between him and Harriet.

Emma is now about to embark on a further attempt to manage other people's lives: having failed to perceive the truth (that Frank is in love with Jane), and having convinced herself of something that is untrue (that Frank loves herself), she seems quite unable to realise that, if only in social terms, a match between Harriet and Frank is out of the question.

Chapter 32 (II, 14)

Emma meets the Eltons and decides that Mrs Elton is a thoroughly vulgar woman.

After her embarrassing and humiliating experience with Mr Elton earlier in the novel, Emma is hardly predisposed to like his new wife. But the narrator clearly endorses her judgement and as the story develops Mrs Elton, whose brash manners contrast sharply with the genuinely ladylike manners of Emma herself (as well as of Jane Fairfax and others), turns out to be the source of much comedy and social satire, aimed at upstart members of the commercial middle class who are eager to use their money to achieve social acceptance but who lack refinement of speech and manner, sensitivity towards others and a sense of social decorum. Jane Austen's sympathies are with the established rural society in contrast to the rapidly changing mercantile and urban world that Mrs Elton represents. By marrying a country clergyman, the latter is, of course, seeking an easy entry into the society of her social betters: although a clergyman's income was not large, his profession and his role in a small community such as Highbury gave him a status that permitted him to mingle with landed proprietors such as Mr Woodhouse and Mr Knightley.

Chapter 33 (II, 15)

There are further glimpses of Mrs Elton, who patronises Jane Fairfax. Mr Knightley tells Emma that, despite her suspicions, he has no interest in marrying Jane Fairfax, whom he finds lacking in 'the open temper which a man would wish for in a wife' (by openness, one of the key concepts of the novel, he means straightforwardness and freedom from guile; its opposite is 'reserve', a word already used more than once in connection with Jane).

Chapter 34 (II, 16)

The Woodhouses give a dinner. In the course of conversation it is mentioned that Jane Fairfax has walked to the post office in the rain, and Emma suspects that she is corresponding secretly with Mr. Dixon.

This is a good example of Emma's characteristic knack, when presented with a piece of evidence, of jumping to a wrong conclusion on account of her preconceived notions: she has made up her mind some time ago, on no other grounds than that the situation appeals to her romantic sense, that Jane is in love with Mr Dixon, and now she does not even contemplate any alternative explanation. Note that Emma's irresponsible imagination blinds her to the nature of what she is considering as likely: if Jane were actually writing to Mr Dixon this would be highly reprehensible and, by the standards of the day, shockingly immoral, for he is a married man. The importance of letter-writing and the receiving of letters in *Emma* has already been commented on. The reason for the removal of Frank from Highbury, which makes the correspondence necessary, only becomes clear as the story unfolds.

Chapters 35 and 36 (II, 17–18)

In these two chapters the scene initiated in Chapter 34 is continued. There is a discussion of Jane's future as a governess. Mr Weston arrives with a letter announcing that Frank will soon return.

The account of the dinner party occupies the last three chapters of the second volume of the novel in the original three-volume form. Like other similar occasions, it allows the development of dialogue which in this case deals largely with Jane Fairfax. There is some unexpectedly sharp social comment on the fate of the unmarried middle-class woman lacking financial security who is forced into the unenviable life of a governess – a fate of which Jane Austen had good reason to be aware. The letter promising Frank's return to Highbury forms an effective 'curtain' to the second volume and points forward to the development of his relationship with Emma and others in the third volume.

Chapter 37 (III, I)

Emma hopes that Frank will not make her a proposal when he returns. The Churchills move to Richmond in Surrey, not far from Highbury; this means that, even if they require Frank to live with them, he will be able to visit his friends in Highbury more readily, and plans for the ball at the Crown are revived.

Chapter 38 (III, 2)

The long-awaited ball takes place. Frank strikes Emma as being 'in an odd humour'. When Mr Elton refuses to dance with Harriet, Mr Knightley steps into the breach and dances with her. At the end of the chapter, Emma dances with Mr Knightley, and in the last few lines of dialogue they agree that they are 'not really so much brother and sister as to make it at all improper' (they are only 'brother and sister' in the very loose sense that Emma's sister has married his brother).

This important chapter offers an excellent example of two of Jane Austen's favourite devices in this novel. First, the social occasion of the ball brings together many of the most important characters and, through the selection (or rejection) of partners for dancing, permits them to be paired off in various combinations. It later turns out that Mr Knightley's gallant coming to the rescue of Harriet, who has been scorned and snubbed by Mr Elton, has far-reaching consequences, though for his part it is only the almost instinctive action of a true gentleman who is considerate for the feelings of others (as Elton emphatically is not). The declaration on the part of Emma and Mr Knightley that they need not regard themselves as merely brother and sister, though light-hearted in this context, also has reverberations throughout the rest of the book.

Second, there is plainly a mystery here - why is Frank Churchill so agitated? - but it is only on a second reading that the full subtlety of Jane Austen's narrative method can be appreciated. The text relates the surface appearance of events and reactions as they might be perceived by Emma or some other observer; but there is a subtext which completely accounts for each detail of Frank's behaviour and his anxiety to see Jane. For a fuller discussion of this point, see Chapter 5, where a specimen passage is discussed.

Chapter 39 (III, 3)

The next day Emma is thinking over the events of the ball when Harriet suddenly arrives in a distressed state, supported by Frank Churchill. She has been out walking and has encountered a party of gypsies whose behaviour has upset and frightened her. By a stroke of luck Frank happened to come along and has rescued her.

Harriet's trifling misadventure, and the nick-of-time rescue by a gallant and handsome gentleman, has a deliberately parodic and mock-heroic quality. But it naturally makes a strong appeal to Emma's romantic tastes: expecting real life to resemble romantic fiction, she quickly sets her imagination busy to build on the promising way in which the two young people have been thrown together by fate or accident. This is clearly another episode with far-reaching implications and promises further complications in the romantic entanglements of the characters. It later turns out to be important that Harriet has been 'rescued' twice in two days (the first time being Mr Knightley's leading her off to dance).

Chapter 40 (III, 4)

Harriet tells Emma that she has now recovered from the pain of her disappointment over Mr Elton, and shows Emma the 'most precious treasures' - a piece of 'court plaister' (sticking plaster) and the stub of a pencil - that are the carefully-guarded mementoes of her love for him. Harriet says that she will never marry but drops a hint that her affections have now been transferred from Mr Elton to another; she does not name this person but remarks that he is 'so superior to Mr Elton'.

This chapter is a logical development from the previous two chapters. Harriet's reference to an unnamed object of her love leaves the door open for more misunderstandings; Emma encourages the ambiguity by agreeing that no name need be mentioned between them. As usual she has jumped to a conclusion, and as usual it is the wrong one: thinking of the most recent episode involving Harriet, the rescue from the gypsies, she assumes that Harriet's love is for Frank Churchill. Psychologically, it is of interest that Emma never for a moment thinks that Harriet may have Mr Knightley in mind, and it is not for another seven chapters that the misunderstanding is sorted out. Emma does not think of Mr Knightley, even though Harriet has abundant reason to feel love and gratitude towards him in her naïve and simple-minded way, because Emma unconsciously thinks of Mr Knightley as belonging to herself.

Chapter 41 (III, 5)

Frank Churchill pays further attentions to Emma, but Mr Knightley suspects him of 'some double dealing in his pursuit' of her as well as of 'some inclination to trifle with Jane Fairfax'. When company are gathered at Hartfield, Frank makes a blunder by letting drop a piece of information that he cannot have learned, as he claims to have done, from the Westons but must have received during his absence from some other source. Later on the same occasion a game is played by forming words with letters of the alphabet: Frank makes the word 'blunder' and shows it to Jane, and when Mr Knightley observes this he has his suspicions confirmed. After the visitors have gone, Mr Knightley tells Emma what he suspects concerning Frank and Jane, but she refuses to believe it.

Mr Knightley's open-minded perceptiveness is here in strong contrast to Emma's wilful blindness. Although he does not yet guess the whole truth concerning Frank and Jane – that they have long been secretly engaged to each other – he is much nearer the truth than anyone else. The reader may suspect that there is an element of unconscious jealousy in his disapproval of Frank's behaviour towards Emma, though it is perfectly true that Mr Knightley has a disinterested concern for Emma's welfare. The word game, like the charades and riddles earlier in the novel, has symbolic overtones: Frank and Jane are playing a kind of real-life game and it is not easy for others to solve the puzzle. Mr Knightley's intelligence and discreet shrewdness, however ('it was his object to see as much as he could, with as little apparent observation'), qualify him as an efficient detective. Frank's success so far in pulling the wool over Highbury eyes makes him overconfident: hence his carelessness in letting drop a piece of gossip that he has learned from one of Jane's letters.

Chapter 42 (III, 6)

It is now mid-June, and a party is organised to visit Donwell Abbey and to pick and eat Mr Knightley's strawberries. Emma is surprised to find Mr Knightley engaged in conversation with Harriet; later she is surprised again when Jane Fairfax leaves the party abruptly and alone, evidently in a state of considerable agitation. Later, Frank Churchill is seen to be in a bad temper.

Again, there is a strong sense of important matters taking place beneath the surface of the narrative. Something has clearly happened to account for Jane's distress and Frank's mood, but what has happened is not made clear. There is a hint of jealousy in Emma's reaction to seeing Mr Knightley and Harriet together.

Chapter 43 (III, 7)

Following the visit to Donwell Abbey, another party is organised, this time to visit Box Hill, the well-known Surrey beauty spot. There, Frank flirts with Emma. When the occasion shows signs of flagging, Emma suggests that they play a game: each person is to tell what he or she is thinking of. When this does not go down very well, she suggests that each person should be required to say 'either one thing very clever, be it prose or verse. . . or two things moderately clever - or three things very dull indeed'. When an opportunity arises for a witticism at the expense of Miss Bates, Emma cannot resist the temptation and Miss Bates' feelings are hurt. There is a discussion on marriage to which Jane Fairfax and Frank Churchill contribute, Frank stating lightheartedly that he wishes Emma to find a wife for him and stipulating only that she be 'very lively' and have hazel eyes; Emma believes he has Harriet in mind, though Harriet does not have hazel eyes (and can hardly be considered very lively), while she herself does. Mr Knightley, when he has an opportunity of speaking in private to Emma, reproaches her for her rudeness to Miss Bates; recognising the justice of what he says, Emma is mortified and ashamed, and on the way home from Box Hill is depressed and tearful.

This chapter presents yet another social occasion, with opportunities for conversation, secret understandings (between Jane and Frank), and misunderstandings (notably on Emma's part). Mr Knightley's reproof shows that, though very fond of Emma, he is far from blind to her shortcomings and is quite prepared to tell her when she has behaved badly; the really reprehensible aspect of her behaviour is that she has been rude to a woman of inferior social status - Miss Bates is not only a thoroughly good-hearted woman, but is in no position to answer back. The games proposed by Emma (one more example of the importance of games and puzzles in this novel) again parallel, as in Chapter 41, the game that Jane and Frank are secretly playing; and there is an obvious irony in Emma's wish to know what each person is thinking, since there are two present who have no intention of proclaiming the truth. Although Emma is able to recognise the truth when Mr Knightley points it out to her (she acknowledges her offence towards Miss Bates), she is apparently blind to the glaring implications of what Frank Churchill says and persists in believing that he has an interest in Harriet even though his words are not at all applicable to Harriet.

Chapter 44 (III, 8)

Unhappy and remorseful, Emma the next day calls on Mis Bates in order to try to make amends for her conduct. She learns that Jane has obtained a position as a governess, arranged for her by Mrs Elton, is soon leaving Highbury, and is evidently unhappy; also that Frank Churchill has left Highbury to return to Richmond.

As in Chapter 38, we are shown the effects but are not yet told the causes; and the question again naturally arises - what has happened to cause Jane and Frank to behave thus? Events are now beginning to move more rapidly, and the reader has to wait only two chapters before having the question answered.

Chapter 45 (III, 9)

Mr Knightley announces that he is going to London to visit his brother. The next day, news arrives that Mrs Churchill has died suddenly, and Emma's reaction is to tell herself that there will now be no serious objection to Frank's marrying Harriet. Jane Fairfax is unwell but rather pointedly refuses the attentions that Emma offers.

Jane Austen is now very busy whetting the reader's curiosity by creating small mysteries that leave questions floating in the reader's mind. Why does Mr Knightley suddenly depart for London? What effect will Mrs Churchill's death have on Frank's future? Is Jane's condition merely a result of her forthcoming departure and the career that awaits her, or is there some other cause?

Chapter 46 (III, 10)

About ten days later, Mrs Weston tells Emma that Frank Churchill has just called on her and has broken the news that he has for some time been engaged to Jane Fairfax (it is now early July and the engagement, 'formed at Weymouth', dates from the previous October). Emma now realises that for the second time her plans for Harriet have gone sadly astray.

The Westons are evidently much concerned that Emma may be deeply upset by the news, and are relieved when she tells them that she has no romantic interest in Frank. Frank's announcement has been precipitated by his learning of Jane's plans to go away as a governess; it has been made possible by the convenient death of Mrs Churchill, who would certainly have objected to such a match, since Jane has no fortune.

This is one of the turning-points of the plot, and much that has been mysterious up to this point is now made clear. Again Emma is forced to recognise that she has been foolish and wrong in supposing Frank to have an interest in Harriet; however, the situation is more complex than she realises, and the full truth of it is still to be revealed.

Chapter 47 (III, 11)

Emma is much concerned at having to break the news to Harriet, and is surprised to find that Harriet already knows it and is not at all affected. When Emma asks her if she did not once care for Frank, to Emma's astonishment she says that she never did. Emma is shattered when she learns that it is Mr Knightley with whom Harriet is in love, and whom Harriet believes to love her. At this point Emma suddenly learns the truth about her own feelings: she loves Mr Knightley herself. After Harriet leaves, Emma is bewildered by this sudden turn of events; on reflection she realises that she has always loved Mr Knightley without being aware of it, and that she has been wrong to try to 'arrange everybody's destiny'. She wishes she had never taken up Harriet, and recognises that she has only herself to blame for encouraging Harriet to think herself worthy of Mr Knightley.

This exchange between Emma and Harriet forms the emotional climax of the story, and the sentence 'It darted through her, with the speed of an arrow, that Mr Knightley must marry no one but herself!' is arguably the most important single sentence in the novel. (It is also exceptional in its use of a vivid image, since Jane Austen in general uses little figurative language.) There is both 'discovery' and 'reversal' in Emma's sudden insight into the truth that Harriet loves not Frank but Mr Knightley. The misunderstanding has originated in a conversation between the two girls in Chapter 40. Emma has not only been imperceptive about the behaviour and true feelings of others, but has lacked self-knowledge; and it is only now that she realises that she herself loves Mr Knightley. Her capacity for misunderstanding and her tendency to jump to conclusions are not yet cured, however: she has only Harriet's word for it that Mr Knightley returns her feelings - and Harriet is hardly a sound judge of character - but Emma immediately takes it for granted that this is so, though there is no substantial evidence to support it.

Chapter 48 (III, 12)

Emma's low spirits and her mood of self-reproach persist. She realises, too late, that instead of taking up Harriet she should have made a friend of Jane Fairfax. The bad weather matches her mood: even though it is July, it is cold, wet, windy and gloomy.

The bitterness of Emma's situation lies partly in the fact, which she fully recognises, that she has helped to create it herself: if her wish to be flattered and admired had not led her to patronise Harriet Smith, Harriet would not now be (as Emma believes she is) beloved by Mr Knightley. Emma's progress in self-knowledge has not yet gone far enough, however, for her to admit to herself the reason why she did not befriend Jane Fairfax, who would have made a much more suitable companion for her, rather than Harriet: she could hardly have felt the same sense of superiority towards Jane, who is intelligent and well-informed and might even have shown Miss Woodhouse to disadvantage at times. The weather is described more fully than usual in this chapter and, as at the beginning of the next chapter, harmonises with the heroine's situation.

Chapter 49 (III, 13)

The weather improves, and Mr Knightley returns from London. To Emma he expresses his indignation at Frank's behaviour; he evidently thinks Emma's heart is broken, but she quickly reassures him, to his great joy and relief, telling him that she has never cared for Frank. Now that this misunderstanding is cleared up, however, another quickly follows: when Mr Knightley tells Emma that there is something he wants to say to her, she, thinking he is about to confess his love for Harriet, discourages him from speaking. When he does at last speak, he tells her that he loves her and makes her a proposal of marriage, which she accepts. She learns that he has been jealous of Frank Churchill, has gone away for that reason, and has returned immediately on hearing the news concerning Frank and Jane.

Again, there is a complete reversal of Emma's feelings in this chapter, made explicit in the opening sentence of the next chapter. The mystery of Mr Knightley's departure for London is now explained: even he is not exempt from error, and has supposed that Frank and Emma might turn out to be in love with each other. The reversal is in fact a double one, for he learns the truth about Emma's feelings just as she learns the truth about his. The proposal and acceptance form the climax of the plot. A notable feature is Jane Austen's refusal to give Emma's speech of acceptance, the reader's romantic and sentimental curiosity being frustrated by the playfully ironic comment: 'What did she say? – Just what she ought, of course. A lady always does.'

Chapter 50 (III, 14)

Emma writes a letter to Harriet breaking the news concerning herself and Mr Knightley (the third time that she has had to perform a similar painful task). She reads a long letter sent by Frank Churchill to Mrs Weston in which he admits that he paid attention to Emma in order to avert suspicion from the truth, makes some bitter comments on Mrs Elton's patronising of

Jane, solves the mystery of the pianoforte (he had made arrangements for its delivery when he went to London with the excuse of getting his hair cut), and states that Jane broke off the engagement on the occasion of the Donwell Abbey party.

The chapter is devoted to two letters - a further reminder of the importance of letter-writing in the period and in Jane Austen's own life, as well as of the fact that the epistolary novel (novel consisting of letters) was a favourite form in the eighteenth century and that some of Jane Austen's own novels began their existence in this form. Frank's letter clears up some further mysteries.

Chapter 51 (III, 15)
Frank's letter reconciles Emma somewhat to his behaviour. Mr Knightley arrives, reads it, and comments on it. There is a discussion between Mr Knightley and Emma concerning their marriage: Emma says that she will not leave her father, and Mr Knightley does not attempt to persuade her otherwise but magnanimously says that he will move into Hartfield when they are married. Emma is still uneasy concerning Harriet.

Chapter 52 (III, 16)
Harriet is to go to London to stay with the John Knightleys. Emma calls on Jane Fairfax and finds Mrs Elton there.

Chapter 53 (III, 17)
A daughter is born to Mrs Weston. The news that Emma and Mr Knightley are to marry is broken to Mr Woodhouse and to the Westons. Mr Weston tells Jane Fairfax, and as soon as Miss Bates hears of it, it spreads through Highbury like wildfire.

Chapter 54 (III, 18)
Mr Knightley tells Emma that Harriet is to marry Robert Martin, and she is very relieved. Emma meets Frank Churchill again at the Westons.

Chapter 55 (III, 19)
The truth about Harriet's parentage comes out at last: she is the 'daughter of a tradesman'. Harriet is married in late September, and Emma about a month later.

Like all Jane Austen's novels, *Emma* ends to the sound of wedding bells: marriage is the traditional conclusion of comedy, and in this instance no fewer than three marriages are involved. (The novel has also begun with a marriage, that of the Westons.) In places the course of events has skated close to a less happy outcome - for example, Harriet's life might conceivably have been permanently blighted by Emma's interference – but as it turns out all find happiness, and none of the marriages promises to shake the fabric of society.

3 THEMES AND ISSUES

3.1 GROWING UP TOWARDS MARRIAGE

On a casual reading *Emma* may not seem to amount to very much. The story is slight: a number of young people who are unmarried when the book opens find partners and marry them some three hundred pages later. Exciting incidents are in distinctly short supply: among the most dramatic episodes in the book are the scenes where one young lady is frightened by meeting some gypsies, and another young lady is rude to an older woman. The mysteries seem trivial: to such questions as 'Who has sent Jane Fairfax a piano?' and 'Why does Jane walk to the post office in the rain?' some readers may feel like responding 'Who cares?'. The setting is restricted, rarely moving outside the confines of a community that is little more than a large village. The number of characters is limited, and the social range also.

To assume that these qualities damagingly limit the interest and significance of the novel, however, is to be guilty of the common fallacy that confuses smallness with narrowness. Jane Austen's limitations were self-imposed. To a niece who was trying to write a novel she said in a letter: 'You are now collecting your People delightfully, getting them exactly into such a spot as is the delight of my life; - 3 or 4 Families in a Country Village is the very thing to work on', and this is close to her own recipe as exemplified in *Emma*. When she was invited to write a novel with a clergyman as the hero, she wrote: 'I think I may boast myself to be, with all possible vanity, the most unlearned and uninformed female who ever dared to be an authoress'; and though we need not take this modest disclaimer at face value (she was, for instance, quite widely read), it does indicate that she set her face firmly against attempting anything that she was not confident of being able to do entirely to her own satisfaction. And her standards, as we know from her persistent satire, from childhood onwards, directed at bad fiction, were very high. Elsewhere she compared her work to that of the miniaturist, referring to 'the little bit (two Inches wide) of Ivory on which I work with so fine a Brush, as produces little effect after much labour'. A good miniature is certainly to be preferred to a bad oil painting that covers an entire wall. But in any case Jane Austen's novels are not merely skilful miniatures: it is in the very nature of the novel that small events can stand for large issues, and a novel outwardly restricted in scope may nevertheless stand as a model or paradigm of universal situations and themes. When Emma is rude to Miss Bates, for instance, the matter is not trivial and Mr Knightley, the wisest character in the book, does not treat it as trivial: important questions of human and social relationships are involved.

It has been said that the theme of *Emma* is growing up; also that its theme is marriage. Though this may look like a difference of opinion, the difference is only apparent, for the two questions are connected. At the beginning of the novel Emma is immature; in the course of it she moves towards maturity, partly as a result of some rather painful experiences in her relationships with other people, partly as a result of Mr Knightley's patient, loving and scrupulous guidance of her developing moral sense. For Jane Austen, self-knowledge – or, to put it more negatively, freedom from illusion and self-deception – was a cardinal attribute of maturity; and it is towards self-knowledge that Emma slowly and uncertainly moves. The self-knowledge that she attains only in the closing portion of the novel involves a recognition that she loves George Knightley; and it is only at this point that she can be said to be ready for marriage. As Jane Austen saw it, the choice of a marriage partner is perhaps the most important and solemn decision that an individual undertakes. Her novels are full of marriages, accomplished or in prospect, and many of them are unsuccessful (in *Emma*, for instance, the implication is that the Eltons' marriage is built on such uncertain foundations as to make it very likely that before long it will produce domestic disharmony).

Emma begins with a marriage, that of the Westons; much of the plot springs from Emma's attempt to arrange a marriage for Harriet Smith; the Eltons offer an example of a marriage made for the wrong reasons (avarice on his side, the wish to rise socially and the fear of being left unmarried on hers); Miss Bates offers a sad example of the fate of the unmarried woman; the John Knightleys have a marriage that consists of mutual tolerance but no real mutual respect; and there are no fewer than three marriages at the end of the book, of which Emma's, as we learn in the closing phrase of the text, leads to 'perfect happiness'. In the course of presenting these various marriages, actual or prospective, Jane Austen explores the social and economic as well as the psychological basis of marriage in her time. For a middle-class woman with no 'fortune' or dowry either inherited or bestowed on her by her parents, and with almost no prospect of earning a living, the alternative to marriage was bleak indeed. She might, as Jane Fairfax intends to, become a governess; but this was to be little better than, and in some respects worse than, a servant in the household of an employer who might be haughty or tyrannical and offered no long-term security. The bitterest passage in *Emma* is the comparison of the profession of governess to the slave-trade (see Chapter 35: Parliament had abolished the slave-trade in 1807, so the subject was topical).

The theme of marriage, and the presentation of a number of marriages none of which is a duplicate of any of the others, thus runs throughout the book. But, as suggested above, it is intimately related to the presentation of Emma's development. When the story opens, Miss Taylor's marriage brings about the first radical change in Emma's life that she can remember. Her situation is rather an unusual one: though the younger daughter, she is 'mistress' of her father's house, since her mother has died in her early infancy and her sister, considerably older than herself, has married many years earlier. As the Woodhouses are socially speaking the first family in Highbury society, this gives her an exceptional role for a girl of twenty, both domestically and socially. Her relationship with her father is also rather a curious one: he is such a nervous and unworldly man that their roles are in effect reversed, and she performs some of the duites of an anxious loving parent solicitous over the welfare of a difficult (and elderly) child. Mr Knightley, as both a relative by marriage and a firm family friend, is something of a father-substitute; but he is nearer to Emma's age than to her father's, and it is more appropriate to think of him as an elder brother. Like an elder brother, he takes responsibility for Emma's moral training and enjoys a frank and good-humoured relationship with her.

Miss Taylor's marriage initiates the action of the novel by leaving Emma for the first time in her life to her own devices; and it is striking that her instinct is to create a situation in which *she* will be the mentor rather than the pupil. It is as if, after being all her life under the tutelage of a governess, she wants to have a taste of that role for herself; and she takes up the dim and empty-headed Harriet, whose chief virtue is that she admires Miss Woodhouse. It is not, of course, an equal friendship; and an equal friendship is not what Emma desires.

At this point we must confront the less admirable, and even objectionable, aspects of Emma's character – aspects of which Jane Austen was well aware, and which indeed she stresses. When she began work on *Emma* she wrote in a letter that she was 'going to take a heroine whom no one but myself will much like'. Thisperhaps overstates the case, as it turned out; but it is certainly true that Emma has had many critics, and it looks as though Jane Austen – who was perfectly capable of creating a heroine such as Elizabeth Bennet in *Pride and Prejudice*, concerning whose attractiveness we can have no reservations – was deliberately setting herself an artistic problem. The very first page of the novel presents her as the spoiled child of a foolish, doting father who is also a wealthy man, and she also has looks and intelligence, as well as social status, to increase her good opinion of herself. The fourth paragraph tells us quite explicitly that she has had 'rather too much her own way' and that she thinks 'a little too well of herself'; moreover, as the opening paragraph states, she has reached the age of twenty 'with very little to distress or vex her'. It is reasonable to guess that this cushioned and cossetted state of affairs will not last, and that Emma will taste distress and vexation before the story is over. Near the end of the book (Chapter 53), Mr Knightley tells her, wittily but candidly, that as a child she was spoiled by Miss Taylor.

Emma, then, is vain, conceited, a spoiled child, and a snob. She takes a dislike to Jane Fairfax for no better reason than that Jane seems to represent a challenge to herself as a beautiful and well-educated girl. More seriously, her self-appointed role as patroness of Harriet Smith and manipulator of her fortunes nearly causes disaster: if Harriet had been a different kind of personality, instead of shedding a few tears at her disappointment over Mr Elton she might have gone off and drowned herself, and if she does not do so it is not Emma's fault. All this, however, is only one side of the picture. Emma has at least one important redeeming feature: her devotion to her father. He is a tiresome and demanding old man, and we might hardly be inclined to blame her if she occasionally lacked patience with him. But she never does: her consideration for him, from start to finish, is admirably unselfish. To this we must add that she is prepared to acknowledge when she is in the wrong, and that, despite her faults (which he is the first to point out) she is obviously admired and loved by Mr Knightley, who is clearly a good judge of character. This makes her a complex character, neither so good as to be bland and uninteresting nor so unattractive as to forfeit our sympathy.

Writing at a time when the Romantic movement in England was well under way (Wordsworth, Coleridge, Scott and Byron had all published poems by the time *Emma* appeared), Jane Austen includes in her novel an attack on the excesses of the imagination allowed to go unchecked by reason and common sense. Emma, we are told, is an 'imaginist': Jane Austen seems to have invented the word, which did not find a permanent place in the language, but it is not difficult to see what she intends by it. Her heroine continually allows herself to be carried away by daydreams and speculations that quickly turn into convictions: she sees not what actually is before her eyes, or what common sense suggests to be likely, but what she would like to be true. Thus she comes to believe, without a shred of evidence, that Harriet must be of gentle birth and therefore (by another leap of reasoning) worthy of a marriage that will raise her to a higher level of society. Such 'insights' in fact constitute a kind of blindness; and Emma is quite unable to see the actualities with which her experience presents her - that Mr Elton, for instance, is anxious to secure her own hand, and that something is going on between Jane Fairfax and Frank Churchill. The critic Mary Lascelles, who has written one of the best studies of Jane Austen, suggests that Emma's illusions originate at least partly in her reading: 'Such a young woman as Emma, so constituted and so circumstanced, could have become acquainted with illegitimacy as an interesting situation, infidelity as a comic incident, only in reading.' Put slightly differently, this means that Emma treats life as if it were a rather bad romantic novel of the kind that Jane Austen delighted to satirise.

It is also true, however, that Emma's own impulsive nature, which she has not yet learned to control through the exercise of reason, impels her to leap to such conclusions and to entertain, for example, the rather startling idea that Jane Fairfax is secretly corresponding with a married man. To this we may add the influence throughout her childhood and adolescence of Miss Taylor, who, although a pleasant and responsible woman, is also inclined to indulge in romantic fancies (it is she who suspects Mr Knightley, again without any real basis, of a romantic interest in Jane Fairfax).

Emma's misunderstandings form the main plot-interest of this comedy of errors that, at least at times, has serious undertones; and her discovery and acceptance of her own mistakes, together with the embarrassment and humiliation this entails, is an important element in her moral growth. In the course of the novel she finds out what the world is really like (the microcosm of Highbury, as already suggested, representing the larger world of experience). In this process of discovery and self-discovery Mr Knightley is an important instrument, ready as he is to show Emma her faults and mistakes. Others who are close to her, such as her father and Mrs Weston, are blind to her follies; those with whom she has a less close relationship, or who are her social inferiors, can hardly do so even if they feel inclined. Mr Knightley is uniquely placed for the task, and well qualified by virtue of his own maturity and solid sense of reality.

Emma's most important mistakes are about personal relationships and especially about love. The way in which the structure of the novel reflects her various errors and misunderstandings will be discussed in more detail in the next chapter, but for the moment we may note that she makes at least five major mistakes. She believes Mr Elton to be in love with Harriet whereas he actually has designs upon herself; she believes Harriet to be in love with Frank Churchill whereas she loves Mr Knightley; she believes the latter to love Harriet, although he loves Emma herself; she believes Jane Fairfax to be pining hopelessly for Mr Dixon, whereas she is secretly engaged to Frank; and perhaps most important of all, she does not realise that she herself is in love with Mr Knightley and cannot bear that he should love or be loved by another. Not all these convictions are entirely groundless; but if Emma does not quite make bricks without straw, she goes a long way beyond what the evidence justifies, and is often capable of entirely misreading the behaviour and intentions of another (as when she can see Mr Elton's flattering attentions as directed only to Harriet).

One of the features of Jane Austen's method is to give variety within the process of repetition, so that although Emma makes a number of mistakes the underlying elements are often different. The mistake over Mr Elton is a case of simple misinterpretation: he makes no attempt to mislead – indeed, to anyone but the over-confident Emma and the easily-led Harriet his behaviour would have been unambiguous, and Mr Knightley at least guesses the truth. When it comes to the errors over Jane Fairfax and Frank Churchill, the situation is different, in that actual dissimulation is involved: these two are playing a game of deliberate deceit, and Emma is not the only one to be hoodwinked (though again Mr Knightley has an inkling of the truth). Another minor error, Emma's short-lived belief that Frank is in love with her, is encouraged by Frank's behaviour, which is again deliberately deceptive. Finally, the knowledge of Mr Knightley's true feelings, and of her own heart, are only arrived at after a more profound kind of self-deception has been thrown off. The tone of these episodes progressively deepens, from the light comedy of Mr Elton's synthetic gallantry and eventual mortification to the sombre depression of Emma's belief (one more error, as it turns out) that she has ruined her own chances of happiness by bringing Harriet and Mr Knightley together, forcing from her the passionate exclamation, 'Oh God! that I had never seen her!' (Chapter 47).

3.2 THE SOCIAL WORLD OF HIGHBURY

It would be an exaggeration to describe Highbury as a microcosm of English society in Jane Austen's day. As we would expect from a writer whose scrupulous concern for realism and accuracy lead her to refuse to deal with any topic of which she does not have first-hand knowledge, the society of Highbury corresponds roughly speaking to her own class and the social levels immediately above and below it. She does not show us the aristocracy (the Churchills, who are great landowners, are heard of but never seen) or the labouring class (though Emma engages in good works for the benefit of the poor cottagers). Apart from a few servants who make only fleeting appearances, all the characters in the novel belong to the middle class – not in itself of course a single class but one involving many levels and discriminations, and including such varieties of occupation, income and status as professional men, landowners and tenant farmers. Even within these groups there are further discriminations: among the professional men, for instance, John Knightley is a London lawyer who is evidently successful and prosperous, Mr Perry a small-town physician, and Mr Elton a clergyman, while the Bates, who are pathetically poor, owe their social status to the fact that Mrs Bates is the widow of a former clergyman.

Jane Austen is thus alert to the significance of class and class-barriers, living as she did in a period in which the concept of class was receiving more attention than ever before (though such words as *rank, order, degree* and *condition* were often used in preference to the word *class*). Under the impact of the French Revolution, the structure of English society came to be examined and questioned with a new consciousness and urgency; and we find a new vocabulary of social class emerging to express these concerns – the term 'higher classes', for instance, seems to have been first used in 1791, and 'working class' and 'middle class' about twenty years later, or at about the same time that *Emma* was written.

If Highbury is a microcosm, then, it is a microcosm of the middle section of English society, which Jane Austen knew well and chose to write about, and which gave her ample opportunities for showing both the divisions of social class and attempts to move from one class to another. It is worth adding that there are several references to the world outside Highbury that remind us that no community, however self-contained, can be sealed off from the rest of the world. London in particular is felt as a near presence: Mr Elton goes there with Harriet's portrait, Frank Churchill goes there to get his hair cut (and to buy a piano), Mr Knightley goes there 'to learn to be indifferent', and the John Knightleys live there and move between their home and Highbury. Outside London, the John Knightleys plan their next seaside holiday (still a relatively new fashion), and Frank lives with the Churchills on their Yorkshire estate, the Eltons meet at Bath, and Mrs Elton originates from Bristol, which was the second city in England until overtaken by the manufacturing towns of the north.

Within Highbury itself, we find a world that reflects a hierarchy based partly on wealth but also on status derived from other sources. (The Martins, for example, are probably much better off than the Bates; but the latter mix with the 'best' society, including the Woodhouses, as the Martins do not, by virtue of the status derived from their relationship to the deceased vicar of the parish.) The most important families are strongly identified with their houses: the Woodhouses with Hartfield, Mr Knightley with Donwell Abbey, the Westons with Randalls. Of lesser importance are other homes such as the Eltons' vicarage, the Martins' farm, the Bates' modest rooms, and so forth. Much of the movement of characters in the novel is from one of these homes to another, and most of the major scenes take place in one or other of them or in some public place such as the Crown Inn or one of the shops in the High Street.

There is also a notable variety of occupations. Mr Knightley is a magistrate and gentleman farmer; Mr Weston, after serving in the army and then spending some twenty years 'engaged in trade', has made enough money to retire in comfort; Mr Elton is a clergyman; Mr John Knightley a lawyer; Mr Perry a doctor; Miss Taylor an ex-governess; Mrs Goddard a teacher; Mr Woodhouse seems never to have worked; nor, for different reasons, has Miss Bates. On the whole, therefore, though this is a fairly affluent (and in some instances a very affluent) society, it is not a leisured one, though it is true that we see nothing of either the urban misery or the rural squalor that was the portion of the vast mass of English people in the period. To such an objection Jane Austen would no doubt have retorted first that she did not intend to write about people of whose lives she knew little or nothing, and second that they would have enabled her to say nothing that she was not able to say with the characters at her disposal. The fact that Shakespeare's tragedies present kings, princes and generals rather than humble life does not limit their universality, and a similar case can be made for Jane Austen.

A further point about Highbury society, and about the scope of the novel as a whole, is that although the action is limited geographically and chronologically, and although many of the issues are hardly of world-shaking importance, *Emma* does include the major dramas of life if only incidentally: birth (Mrs Weston's daughter), the rearing of children (the John Knightleys, as well as references to Emma's own upbringing), love and marriage, and death (that of Mrs Churchill). Jane Austen did not, like Scott or Tolstoy, set herself to depict the history of nations; but within the province of private individual lives she touches on a wide range of experience.

The society of Highbury, then, forms a hierarchy, with the Woodhouses at the top and the other characters in the novel ranged at different distances beneath them. (Only the Churchills are superior to the Woodhouses in status, and they are never seen.) It is not, however, a hierarchy that is rigidly and permanently fixed. A limited degree of class mobility had always been possible in English society, and during Jane Austen's lifetime the pace of change was accelerated. The great agents of mobility were money and marriage, very often in combination; and *Emma* offers us some case-studies in upward mobility of various kinds. (The Bates, in contrast, have come *down* in the world.) The Coles, for instance, who give a dinner-party in Chapter 26, represent the type of *nouveaux riches* who were to become much more common in Victorian middle-class society and to be duly satirised by Dickens, Trollope, and other novelists. We learn in Chapter 25 that they are 'of low origin' and 'only moderately genteel', but as a result of being engaged 'in trade' they have, like Mr Weston, prospered and have begun to change their style of living: having lived quietly during their early years in Highbury, they are now 'in fortune and style of living, second only to the family at Hartfield', and Emma and her father have no scruples about dining with them. Their saving grace is that they are 'very good sort of people - friendly, liberal, and unpretending', and this distinguishes them from, and makes them more readily acceptable than, Mrs Elton, whose origins are similar.

More important than this rising in the ranks through earned wealth, which permits an improved style of living, is the change in status that comes about as a result of a marriage alliance. We may divided the characters in the novel into two groups: those whose social status is fixed, and those who are at least potentially mobile. In the first group are, for example, Mr Woodhouse and Mr Knightley, and on a lower level such families as the Bates and the Martins. In the second group are Harriet Smith, Jane Fairfax, and Augusta Hawkins (later Mrs Elton). We may notice that the members of the second group belong to the younger generation, also that they are unmarried. Emma herself, of course, also possesses these attributes, but her social position is assured and, as she is well aware, she has no need to marry in order to secure either respect or financial security. (See her comments on the subject in Chapter 10.)

Harriet has no 'fortune', but her great point of interest, for Emma at least, is that her family origins are unknown. Emma chooses to believe that Harriet is the illegitimate daughter of someone high in the social scale - a princess turned into a goose-girl, as it were - but the revelation at the end of the novel that she is 'the daughter of a tradesman' puts Emma's romantice notion that she had 'the blood of gentility' firmly in its place. Emma schemes to marry off Harriet to a husband beyond her social expectations - first to Mr Elton, then (even more ambitiously) to Frank Churchill - and is quite prepared to believe that Mr Knightley would consider Harriet a suitable wife. Harriet's eventual union with Robert Martin has nothing startling about it but is suitable in every way, including the respective social positions of the two young people.

Jane Fairfax succeeds, as Harriet does not, in making a marriage that raises her in the social scale: in her case, the Cinderella story comes true, and the poor girl, with neither wealth nor family connections to help her, and with the grim prospect of a life of ill-paid drudgery as a governess, marries the handsome young man who is the heir (if not exactly the son) of a great family with large estates. We feel that Jane deserves her success, beautiful and talented as she is; and it must be quickly added that there is in her no taint of ambition or calculating worldliness: she genuinely loves Frank, and is indeed better than he deserves.

As for 'the charming August Hawkins', whose 'independent fortune' is such a successful bait for Mr Elton, she too succeeds in her ambition to marry well but offers a very different case from Jane Fairfax: Mr Elton's rapid courtship, related sardonically in Chapter 22 in a single brilliant sentence, succeeds because she is 'so very ready to have him'. Her fortune has been derived from her father's business ventures, and she represents a class eager to secure the prestige of a higher position in society overnight. No doubt she has gone to Bath, a fashionable resort, with the express purpose of finding a husband. The Eltons' match is a textbook instance of the kind of mutually beneficial alliance common at the time: in return for her money, which he badly needs, Mr Elton offers his bride the status derived from the position of a clergyman of the Established Church in a small community in which the church was the centre of communal life, and the vicar enjoyed a position that bore no relation to his income.

As the example of the Eltons shows, and as Jane Austen was only too aware from personal observation, marriage in the period was not just a matter of love or personal compatibility but often involved the transfer of capital and adjustments, minor or major, of social status. Modern views of Jane Austen reject the earlier impression of her as merely retailing, more or less amiably, small-town gossip and domestic trivialities, and see her as fully conscious, in an entirely hard-headed way, of the way in which social and individual life was affected by considerations of wealth and status. The point is nicely made by W. H. Auden in his *Letters from Iceland:*

> You could not shock her more than she shocks me;
>   Beside her Joyce seems innocent as grass.
> It makes me most uncomfortable to see
>   An English spinster of the middle-class
>   Describe the amorous effects of 'brass',
> Reveal so frankly and with such sobriety
> The economic basis of society.

If *Emma* is a love story, a study of growing up, and a comedy of errors and illusions, it is also a picture of 'The economic basis of society' – not, of course, in the abstract or generalised terms of a sociologist or historian, but in the concrete, vividly realised and dramatic terms of a great novelist.

4 TECHNIQUES

4.1 PLOT AND STRUCTURE

Emma stands at the centre of the novel to which she gives her name: the opening and closing sentences refer to her, and there is nothing of importance between them that does not have a direct or indirect bearing on her experience and development. This gives the novel a remarkable quality of unity and concentration: unlike the Victorian novel of a generation or two later, with its proliferating sub-plots, it is held together by presenting the world as the heroine sees it and excluding almost everything else.

'Plot' is in fact an ambiguous word in relation to *Emma*, which not only has a plot in the usual literary sense of a series of events linked by causation and leading the reader to ask questions that are answered in the fullness of time, but also involves a great deal of plotting in the other sense of scheming, planning, and concealment of the truth. Emma plots to marry off Harriet to one and then another unsuspecting young man; meanwhile, a more serious and genuine conspiracy is taking place as Frank and Jane conceal their engagement from their relations and friends. The novel also bristles with minor examples of plotting in this second sense, as when Mr Elton schemes to marry Emma, or Frank makes the secret present of a piano to Jane.

On the basis of this central idea of a heroine busily plotting but quite unaware of the plots of others, Jane Austen has structured a novel that is a remarkable example of narrative economy and skill. More than any other full-length novel in English, perhaps, *Emma* is an example of total relevance: not a chapter, and hardly a sentence, of the novel fails to have a bearing on the main purpose. No detail is given simply for its own sake or merely as part of the furnishing of realistic fiction: when Frank Churchill gets his hair cut, or borrows a pair of scissors from Miss Bates, these trivial matters have a definite function in the story.

It is not, however, a function that is always immediately apparent; and it can be said of *Emma* that it is a novel impossible to understand fully on a single reading. On a second reading many small touches are seen in an entirely different light: with the hindsight afforded by knowledge of the outcome, a different meaning is attached to countless examples of behaviour and speech from that which was given to them on a first reading. *Emma* has been compared to a detective story, and it certainly has in common with that genre of fiction the incorporation of a great many clues within the narrative that most readers are likely to miss, or to misinterpret, as they read, though on reflection or reperusal their true meaning becomes plain. Like a good detective-story writer, Jane Austen plays fair with the reader: the evidence is there for him to interpret correctly if he is able to do so. Emma herself may be compared to a hopelessly incompetent detective who either misses the clues entirely or, when she does see them, misinterprets them. Mr Knightley, on the other hand, is more adept at making correct deductions - he guesses, for instance, that there is more than meets the eye in Frank Churchill's relationship with Jane Fairfax - though even he is blind to much of what is going on.

In an excellent essay on Jane Austen included in *Critical Essays on Jane Austen*, (ed. Brian Southam, 1968), Rachel Trickett has described *Emma* as 'the most original and skilfully planned' of Jane Austen's novels and has described the three-part nature of the 'formal structure':

> The action moves in three parts like the acts of a play, the first two centring on the suitors favoured by Emma for Harriet. . . the last. . . reveals to Emma her real feelings and to us the true nature of the work. . .

The novel thus has the distinct beginning, middle and end that Aristotle (who had read no novels) praised in a well-made play. It has already been suggested that these divisions roughly correspond to the three volumes in which the novel was originally published and, we may suppose, originally conceived. Thus Emma learns the truth about Mr Elton's intentions in Chapter 15, feels remorse for her mistake in Chapter 16, and learns that Mr Elton is leaving Highbury for a time and informs Harriet of the true state of affairs in Chapter 17 - these chapters bringing us very near the end of the first volume. In Chapter 18, the last of Volume I, with Mr Elton out of the way, Frank Churchill becomes an object of attention; this chapter is thus a bridge leading to the second volume, where Frank is to figure importantly. In the first two chapters of the second volume (Chapters 19 and 20), Jane Fairfax receives more attention than ever before, preparing us for her important role in the remainder of the book. By the end of the second volume, Emma's short-lived interest in Frank as a potential lover for herself is almost over, and the second and third chapters of the third volume (Chapters 38 and 39) lay the ground for the misunderstanding between Emma and Harriet concerning the latter's affections.

All this may seem to suggest that there is something excessively formal, even mechanical, about the structure of the novel; but nothing could be further from the truth. As Rachel Trickett points out, the greatest formality of structure is found in the 'simple comedy of self-deceit' in the first part of the book; 'the middle section develops more naturally and the denouement, though a perfect example of comic reversal and comic timing, is so well contained within the realistic atmosphere of the preceding part that it illustrates exactly [the] interplay of formal unity with the wider effect of reality. . .'. For Jane Austen the structure is only a means to an end; the 'effect of reality' and truth to experience are paramount; and the unrivalled excellence of the book lies in its marriage of formal perfection with wisdom and truth. Its subtlety, moreover, derives from the fact that so much is going on between the lines: as W. J. Harvey has aptly said, 'The written novel contains its unwritten twin whose shape is known only by the shadow it casts' - to which we may add that both shapes, that of the 'written' and that of the 'unwritten' novel, perfectly express Jane Austen's intentions.

4.2 NARRATIVE POINT OF VIEW

W. J. Harvey's comment, quoted above, raises the question of point of view, since the fact that so much in the novel is unstated, or incompletely stated, arises from the fact that the reader is given not the whole truth but little more than Emma herself sees - and she, it is clear, is an unusually unreliable observer. (There is a significant ambiguity in the word 'sees' as used here: the verb commonly possesses two related but distinct senses, as in 'I see a dog' and 'I see your point'; and in her presentation of Emma, Jane Austen virtually puns on the word, since Emma 'sees' without 'seeing'. Part of Emma's self-discovery in Chapter 47 is that she has been guilty of 'blindness', and it is instructive to study the text with special attention to words such as 'seeing' and 'seeming', which are numerous.)

The choice of point of view is one of the most important preliminary decisions that a novelist has to make, and a large part of the effect of a novel will depend on what decision is made. In *Emma* Jane Austen's problem was to win the reader's sympathy for a heroine who often behaves foolishly and who can be bossy, inconsiderate and snobbish. An obvious way of securing sympathy for Emma would be the use of a first-person narrative such as Charlotte Brontë uses in *Jane Eyre* and Charles Dickens in *Great Expectations:* Dickens' hero (Pip), like Emma, has some unattractive qualities, but the fact that his story constitutes a kind of confession and that he exposes his own weaknesses so candidly helps the reader to accept and forgive him. But Jane Austen never wrote a novel using the first-person narrator: the nearest she comes to this method of story-telling is in the letters she incorporates verbatim into her narrative (e.g. Frank Churchill's long letter given in Chapter 50). No doubt she was unwilling to forgo the opportunity for objective commentary that she occasionally likes to make but that is impossible in a first-person narrative: the opening paragraph of *Emma*, to take an obvious instance, could not be accommodated in such a narrative. On the other hand, Emma seen completely objectively, as she might be if depicted by a third-person narrator, would be an unsympathetic figure. The critic Wayne Booth has put the point forcefully: 'Seen from the outside, Emma would be an unpleasant person, unless, like Mr Woodhouse and Knightley, we knew her well enough to infer her true worth'.

Jane Austen's solution is the only logical one, though at the time it showed great boldness and originality. She casts her novel in the form of a third-person narrative, but rather than using the 'omniscient' narrator usually favoured she carefully and consistently limits the scope of what is narrated so that it corresponds almost exactly to what Emma sees and thinks. As a result, the reader finds himself not merely observing Emma but seeing the world through her eyes and, in all probability, making some of the same errors that she makes; this again helps to win our sympathy for the heroine, since we are unlikely to blame her severely for mistakes that we too have committed. Emma's world is very largely the world of the novel, and her angle of vision dominates every scene in which she appears – which amounts to nearly every scene in the book, since we rarely or never see the other characters for any length of time except in Emma's presence (Frank Churchill and Jane Fairfax, for example, are never shown alone together).

Emma's specific, and often erroneous, way of perceiving what is going on around her is fairly obvious in her speeches; what is not quite so obvious is that it also colours the portions of the text that, superficially at least, appear to be more or less objective narrative. Thus, when she says to Harriet in Chapter 4, referring to Mr Elton:

> 'He seems to me to be grown particularly gentle of late. I do not know whether he has any design of ingratiating himself with either of us, Harriet. . .but it strikes me that his manners are softer than they used to be. If he means anything, it must be to please you.'

we recognise this, at any rate on a second reading, as a characteristically false deduction on Emma's part: the leap from 'either of us' to 'must be to please you' is unjustified and, as it later turns out, untrue, and the speech shows Emma in the actual process of spinning fantasy. Two chapters later, when Emma is drawing a portrait of Harriet, we read:

> . . .there was no doing anything with Mr Elton fidgetting behind her and watching every touch. She gave him credit for stationing himself where he might gaze and gaze again without offence. . .

Here we have exactly the same kind of misunderstanding, but this time it is embedded within what appears to be an objective narrative and endorsed, as it were, by the narrator's voice – a voice that is confident, witty, ironic and elegant, and that we may feel inclined to identify with that of Jane Austen. However, though the pronouns are now third- rather than first-person ('she' rather than 'I'), the point of view, even the physical position, and the false deduction are entirely Emma's. It would not be going too far to suggest that this kind of narrative amounts to a version of Emma's own thoughts, without such indications as quotation marks or 'she said to herself'. It is essential to Jane Austen's method that what she refers to in Chapter 41 as Emma's 'errors of imagination' should be communicated to the reader through Emma's mind and not by any more perceptive or more objective narrator. (Consider, for instance, how entirely different the novel would be if the story were narrated by Mr Knightley.) With great ingenuity, the novelist presents simultaneously two views of reality: Emma's and the true one. The former is explicit, the latter implicit and only to be interpreted by an exceptionally acute reader or on a second reading.

One corollary of the method is that none of the other characters can be known as fully as Emma herself or seen from the inside as Emma is. In this respect Jane Austen's third-person narrative shares the one-sidedness we associate with autobiographical narratives such as those of Jane Eyre or Pip. This can be seen very clearly by considering the presentation of Jane Fairfax. To quote Wayne Booth again:

> . . .Emma must shine supreme. It is not only that the slightest glance inside Jane's mind would be fatal to all of the author's plans for mystification about Frank Churchill, though this is important. The major problem is that any extended view of her would reveal her as a more sympathetic person than Emma herself.

Jane Austen was well aware of these dangers, and she keeps Jane Fairfax, who on her first introduction looks as if she might be fully developed as a foil to Emma, in the background, so that we see and hear relatively little of her. An omniscient narrator could hardly have avoided giving the game away concerning Jane and Frank, as well as making more explicit such matters as Mr Knightley's jealousy prompted by Frank's attentions to Emma. Jane Austen's method in this novel is an admirable example of technique perfectly adapted to the psychological and moral purposes of the fiction.

4.3 METHODS OF CHARACTERISATION

Our total impression of a novel's characters derives from many sources: from what they say, what they do, what other characters say about them, and what the narrator tells us about them. Nor is it, especially with an ironist like Jane Austen, a simple matter of totting up items of information: the reader is constantly called upon to exercise his own judgement, to relate one piece of information (which may be a lie or a delusion) to another, to bring a healthy scepticism to the evidence offered. Thus, when Mrs Elton declares 'I never compliment', everything we know about her, including the context of that remark (in Chapter 38), makes us disinclined to take it at face value. It still tells us something about Mrs Elton, of course; but what it tells us is not what it appears to be telling us.

Jane Austen is unlike many novelists in that her characters are seen largely, indeed almost exclusively, as individuals leading emotional and moral lives and as social beings, but hardly at all as physical presences. Whereas Dickens, for instance, will devote whole paragraphs to a graphic account of the appearance, gait, gestures, vocal attributes and other idiosyncratic features of his characters, Jane Austen is very sparing of description (a generalisation that applies, incidentally, to places and weather conditions as well as to people: the brief description of the grounds of Donwell Abbey in Chapter 42, and the allusions to the weather in Chapters 48 and 49, are the rare exceptions). Although the opening sentence of the novel tells us that Emma is 'handsome', we learn little more of her physical appearance except that her eyes are 'hazel'. If we try to visualise other characters, such as Mr Knightley or Miss Bates, we find that there is very little basis in the text for us to work on.

A glance at the passage in Chapter 2 in which Miss Bates is introduced to the reader illustrates very clearly the marked bias of Jane Austen's descriptions. Apart from being told that she was not 'handsome', we learn nothing of Miss Bates as a visible presence: whether she is tall or short, fat or thin, we simply do not know, and for Jane Austen it is unimportant. The emphasis of the passage is on the generalised qualities that can be deduced from innumerable small instances of behaviour and in the key sentences

> And yet she was a happy woman, and a woman whom no one named without good-will. It was her own universal good-will and contented temper which worked such wonders

the most important words are the abstract nouns 'good-will' and 'temper'. Miss Bates' importance is in exemplifying moral and ethical qualities, in this instance qualities that command our admiration: as Mr Knightley puts it in Chapter 29, 'She is a standing lesson of how to be happy'. At the same time, though Miss Bates is not a visible presence, she is emphatically an audible one, and her presentation is so memorable because, after this introduction, it is largely through the dramatic medium of her own monologues.

A few examples from the novel will illustrate the various components referred to above by means of which an impression of a character is created. The opening lines of the first chapter, like the introductory account of Miss Bates already cited, are in the 'voice' of the narrator, whom many readers will readily identify with the novelist. At the other end of the novel, the account of Mr Knightley's proposal to Emma in Chapter 49, with its audacious refusal to give Emma's reply, clearly has the same status. As the previous section of this chapter has suggested, however, this kind of statement is relatively rare as third-person narratives go, since so much of the narrative is coloured by Emma's own point of view.

Our placing of what the characters say about each other will depend very much, of course, on our assessment of the speaker, just as it does in real life. Such characters as Mrs Elton and Harriet Smith hardly strike us as sound or reliable judges of character - the former because of her obvious prejudices and her wish to impress others, the latter because of her limitations of intellect and experience. At the other extreme we have Mr Knightley, who is not merely destined to be Emma's husband but serves throughout the novel as the representative and voice of good sense and shrewd judgement. Mr Knightley represents maturity in contrast to Emma's immaturity. To be always in the right is not necessarily attractive, though it may be an admirable quality, and one critic has found him 'pompous, condescending, and a bore' (Angus Wilson). This seems, however, to overlook the fact that he has a pleasant dry wit (as when he politely but firmly puts Mrs Elton in her place), as well as the fact that he is not infallible (he is wrong about Emma's feelings towards Frank Churchill, and very humanly wrong - misled by his feelings rather than his intellect).

In *Emma*, however, the main source of information about the characters comes not from authorial comment or from the statements (true or false) of others but from their own mouths. Jane Austen does not present character and dialogue with the kind of extravagant eccentricity and delight in the grotesque that we find in Smollett or Dickens, and her social world is narrower than that of most novelists; but she discriminates very finely (in both senses of the adverb) between different speakers, and each of the major characters is endowed with his or her own distinctive mode of speech - a mode that is (again as in real life) revelatory of character. Alexander Pope said of Shakespeare that

> every single character. . .is as much an Individual, as those in Life itself; it is as impossible to find any two alike. . .had all the Speeches

> been printed without the very names of the Persons, I believe one might have applied them with certainty to every speaker. . .

No less is true of Jane Austen's characterisation and art in *Emma.*

One factor on her side was the importance attached in her age to 'correctness' and 'propriety' in the spoken language, which made any departure from the desired norm easy to recognise and to judge. Though class differences as revealed through speech are far from having disappeared from the English social scene, they are less prominent now, and less confidently judged, than they were two hundred years ago. This correlation of 'good' speech (including such matters as choice of vocabulary as well as accent and pronunciation) with social status was only one aspect of a situation manifested on many levels; as the historian Harold Perkin has said:

> Differential status was part of the given, unquestioned environment into which men were born, and they proclaimed it by every outward sign: manner, speech, deportment, dress, liveried equipage, size of house and household, the kind and quantity of the food they ate.

Jane Austen makes some of her social points through references to such matters as equipage and size of house and household - we learn who has a carriage, who has two, and who has none; also that, for instance, the Coles increase the number of their servants and build an extension to their house as they grow rich - but she makes far more through dialogue.

Something of the range of spoken styles can be seen by comparing the speech of Mr Knightley with that of Mrs Elton. We are told explicitly in Chapter 51 that Mr Knightley uses 'plain, unaffected, gentleman-like English. . .even to the woman he was in love with', and his speech is obviously an index to his character as a plain, unaffected, and completely consistent gentleman. For Jane Austen, who tended to associate the traditional virtues with rural life and often regarded the city as a source of corruption and decadence, it is important that he is a *country* gentleman: while he could presumably afford to put a manager in charge of his estate and live the life of a man of fashion in London, he prefers to stay in Highbury and manage it himself. To quote another historian, F. M. L. Thompson:

> Honour, dignity, integrity, considerateness, courtesy and chivalry were all virtues essential to the character of a gentleman, and they all derived in part from the nature of country life.

This is very close to being an account of Mr Knightley's own character, and it is not far-fetched to regard his surname as symbolic: he represents for Jane Austen a modern version of the knightly virtues (his Christian name is that of England's patron saint).

Mrs Elton represents a different class with very different values, and it comes as no surprise that her speech is as different as possible from the 'plain, unaffected' language of Mr Knightley. It has a kind of tawdry modishness thoroughly in keeping with her character: she resorts to slang, to fashionable foreign phrases, to familiarities such as calling her husband 'Mr E' and referring to Mr Knightley as 'Knightley' (to Emma's high indignation: 'never seen him in her life before, and call him Knightley!'), and is occasionally ungrammatical. For once Emma's judgement is sound when she comments on Mrs Elton's manners:

> A little upstart, vulgar being, with her Mr E., and her *caro sposo*, and her resources, and all her airs of pert pretension and underbred finery.

Again, we find the qualities of speech to be an accurate guide to character and values.

While the more important themes of the novel are developed through the kind of conversational exchanges we call dialogue - as in the serious conversations between Emma and Mr Knightley - a character such as Mrs Elton delivers what is essentially a monologue: a one-man (or one-woman) exhibition which needs and indeed tolerates little in the way of intervention by others. The critic D. W. Harding has noted that monologue, as opposed to 'the equal give and take of conversation', often serves the purpose of satire and caricature in Jane Austen, and that *Emma* offers more than one example of 'the isolation of a speaker for purposes of caricature'. The other outstanding example is, of course, Miss Bates; but she is viewed as tolerantly, even affectionately, as Mrs Elton is viewed critically and destructively. The speeches of Miss Bates have a Shakespearean richness and vividness of detail (an obvious comparison is with Juliet's nurse in *Romeo and Juliet*). A notable feature is that she is in effect given the floor to herself even when other people's contibutions to the conversation have evidently been made: see the monologue in Chapter 38 beginning 'So very obliging of you!', where the interventions of others are suppressed, though they can readily be deduced.

4.4 LANGUAGE AND STYLE

Jane Austen's prose is a highly flexible instrument, adapting itself readily to the shifting purposes of her fiction and to the modulations of tone that occur not only from one episode or passage to another but sometimes from sentence to sentence, and even (as we shall see below) in mid-sentence. The variety of her dialogue has been referred to in the preceding section, and no less variety is to be found in the non-dialogue portions of the novel.

Consider, for instance, the following brief extracts:

(a) Jane Fairfax was an orphan, the only child of Mrs Bates's youngest daughter. (Chapter 20)
(b) She had never boasted either beauty or cleverness. Her youth had passed without distinction, and her middle of life was devoted to the care of a failing mother, and the endeavour to make a small income go as far as possible. (Chapter 3)
(c) Human nature is so well disposed towards those who are in interesting situations, that a young person, who either marries or dies, is sure of being kindly spoken of. (Chapter 22)
(d) The evening of this day was very long, and melancholy, at Hartfield. The weather added what it could of gloom. A cold stormy rain set in, and nothing of July appeared but in the trees and shrubs, which the wind was despoiling, and the length of the day, which only made such cruel sights the longer visible. (Chapter 49)
(e) It was a sweet view - sweet to the eye and the mind. English verdure, English culture, English comfort, seen under a sun bright, without being oppressive. (Chapter 42)

Brief and to the point, with not a word wasted, (a) communicates facts without commentary in a prose style that has not dated at all - indeed, the sentence might have been written yesterday - and makes no attempt to generalise from the particular case. While also referring to an individual, (b) makes use of abstractions (*beauty, cleverness, youth*, etc.) and we may have the sense that Miss Bates is, among other things, a case-study of a sadly common type. There is a poise and deliberateness in the prose that derives from the eighteenth-century writers whom Jane Austen admired, such as Dr Johnson, and which is seen most obviously in the antitheses ('either beauty or cleverness', 'Her youth. . .her middle of life'). Without being exaggeratedly artificial - there is, for instance, a colloquial quality in the concluding phrases quoted - this is a more formal prose than (a), and the extract in fact forms part of a lengthy portrait that amounts to a kind of set-piece. Like (a), (c) is the opening sentence of a chapter; unlike (a), it has an epigrammatic and sententious quality, and a breadth of reference, that make for formality. It is also ironic, the irony being directed not (as it usually is) at individuals but at 'human nature' in general. With (d) we encounter a different kind of prose, and a kind relatively rare in Jane Austen but striking and effective when it appears. Its purpose is to convey not facts or generalised intellectual attitudes but feelings about a specific occasion, in this instance the effect of weather upon mood. The subject, and the use of such words as 'melancholy', 'gloom' and 'cruel', might be found in such pre-Romantic poets as Cowper, whom Jane Austen read and admired (and whom she quotes in Chapter 41 of *Emma*), and in her

Romantic contemporaries Wordsworth, Coleridge and Byron. (e) presents a different scene, and one more in harmony with Jane Austen's characteristic mood: the view of well-ordered lawns, gardens and fields ('verdure' and 'culture') on the Donwell Abbey estate expresses the values of a way of life in which 'nature', like human passions, is kept under control, and the prose, while moving forward with a naturalness that seems to echo the inflections of the speaking voice, is also firmly under control (as in the precision of the final phrase).

Three particular features of Jane Austen's style in *Emma* may be noted. As in her other novels, she makes extensive use of abstract nouns, and of their related adjectives and adverbs, to denote human attributes, both desirable and undesirable. In this respect she is again the heiress of the eighteenth-century moralists and essayists; as C. S. Lewis has said, these are 'the great abstract nouns of the classical English moralists'. Another critic, Arnold Kettle, has pointed out that 'Each word has a precise and unambiguous meaning based on a social usage at once subtle and stable.' One example of such a word in *Emma* is *elegance*, which is used in connection with Jane Fairfax and for Jane Austen represents something much more than a standard of personal appearance or external behaviour: elegance is also a mental quality, involving a due sense of propriety and decorum, of what is appropriate and inappropriate in a given situation. Mrs Elton, in contrast, has *ease* - a forwardness or self-confidence unjustified by circumstances - but lacks elegance. For Emma herself, *cleverness* is a key concept: she is not well educated, being too volatile to pursue a regular course of study with perseverance, but is naturally quick and intelligent - a quality that, in the lack of the restraint that is given by reason and experience, leads to her wild flights of imagination (another key word). The adjective *clever* is used in the opening sentence of the novel, and we are also told that Emma is 'the cleverest of her family'; a statement that our knowledge of Mr Woodhouse and Isabella Knightley will hardly lead us to contradict.

Another stylistic feature of importance in *Emma* is the kind of interior monologue or inner speech that enables Jane Austen to give the reader an insight into her heroine's unspoken thoughts and unexpressed feelings. This represents, historically speaking, a notable innovation, since Jane Austen here devises a mode of narration that we associate more readily with such modern writers as Virginia Woolf. An extract from the beginning of Chapter 16 will show how smoothly she modulates into this form of narrative:

> The hair was curled, and the maid sent away, and Emma sat down to think and be miserable. - It was a wretched business, indeed! - Such an overthrow of every thing she had been wishing for! - Such a

> development of every thing most unwelcome! – Such a blow for Harriet! – That was the worst of all. . .

The first sentence, which sets the scene economically, belongs to the 'voice' of the narrator; but from 'It was a wretched business. . .' we seem to be given a verbalisation of Emma's own thoughts, even though they are not placed within quotation marks and do not employ the first person singular. We can, if we choose, reconstruct the phrases that Emma might have used in 'speaking' to herself in her solitude, along the lines of 'What a wretched business it is!' Jane Austen avoids this kind of direct monologue, which is bound to seem rather artificial in a realistic novel: her heroine is not a Shakespearean protagonist who can step to the front of the stage and deliver a soliloquy. Her method is to merge inner speech with objective narrative; at the same time the distinctive nature of the former is signalled by various devices such as (in the example quoted) the series of exclamations and the colloquial phrase 'a wretched business'.

Another example from later in the novel exhibits similar qualities. This time Emma's emotions have been aroused by Mr Knightley's reproof after her rudeness to Miss Bates at Box Hill:

> The truth of his representation there was no denying. She felt it at her heart. How could she have been so brutal, so cruel to Miss Bates! – How could she have exposed herself to such ill opinion in any one she valued! And how suffer him to leave her without saying one word of gratitude, of concurrence, of common kindness! (Chapter 43)

Again, Emma's self-reproach is dramatised and not merely stated: we seem to share her inner experience, almost to hear her private thoughts, though again the inner speech blends unobtrusively with the narrative (the first two sentences quoted do not seem to belong to Emma's reflections but to be stated by the impersonal narrator).

Finally, the syntax of Jane Austen's prose in *Emma* is often dramatic, the twists and turns of her sentences corresponding to the changes of attitude and feeling that are in question. Here, from Chapter 15, is a single sentence running to 125 words – it is followed, in striking contrast, by one of four words – in which Mr Elton's totally unexpected proposal takes place:

> To restrain him as much as might be, by her own manners, she was immediately preparing to speak with exquisite clamness and gravity of the weather and the night; but scarcely had she begun, scarcely had they passed the sweep-gate and joined the other carriage, than she found her subject cut up – her hand seized – her attention demanded, and Mr Elton actually making violent love to her: availing himself of the precious opportunity, declaring sentiments which must be already

> well known, hoping - fearing - adoring - ready to die if she refused him; but flattering himself that his ardent attachment and unequalled love and unexampled passion could not fail of having some effect, and in short, very much resolved on being seriously accepted as soon as possible.

The sentence begins calmly and deliberately, and as far as the first semi-colon everything seems to be perfectly under control - a control manifested, for example, by the elegant antitheses 'calmness and gravity', 'the weather and the night'. The quality of the syntax is also that of the dramatic situation: up to that point Emma has control of it. But, with the word 'but', things begin to get out of hand; and there is a new urgency in the repetition of 'scarcely'. Within a couple of lines the sentence, like Emma's 'subject' of conversation, is interrupted or 'cut up', and flies to fragments: the stately phrases and clauses give way to short phrases and the dramatic punctuation of dashes. From 'availing himself' the diction echoes that which we are to suppose Mr Elton himself to have used in his declaration to Emma, and such hypocritical sentiments as 'ready to die', like such clichés as 'precious opportunity', are the objects of satire. The comedy of the situation is that Mr Elton, knowing he will be alone with Emma for only a very short time, is forced to gabble off a lengthy proposal that has no doubt been carefully rehearsed; and this breathless quality is conveyed through this long sentence, the unexpected change of direction of which mirrors the astonishment felt by Emma and the complete reversal of her ideas that Mr Elton's behaviour forces upon her. It is a sentence that, like so much of Jane Austen's prose, displays uncommon skill and artistry and repays the closest possible study.

5 SPECIMEN PASSAGE AND COMMENTARY

5.1 SPECIMEN PASSAGE

Jane Austen's art in *Emma* is one of subtle technique and flexible style: it is hardly an exaggeration to say that not a word is superfluous and every sentence and paragraph, however apparently unimportant, plays its part in the presentation of story, character and theme. The followng analysis of a single short passage is offered as an illustration of these qualities and as an example that may be helpful to the student called upon to undertake a similar exercise. The passage occurs at the beginning of Chapter 38: the company is assembling for the ball at the Crown. The lines are numbered here for ease of reference.

> No misfortune occurred, again to prevent the ball. The day approached, the day arrived; and, after a morning of some anxious watching, Frank Churchill, in all the certainty of his own self, reached Randall's before dinner, and every thing was safe.
>
> No second meeting had there yet been between him and Emma. The room at the Crown was to witness it; – but it would be better than a common meeting in a crowd. Mr. Weston had been so very earnest in his entreaties for her early attendance, for her arriving there as soon as possible after themselves, for the purpose of taking her opinion as to the propriety and comfort of the rooms before any other persons came, that she could not refuse him, and must therefore spend some quiet interval in the young man's company. She was to convey Harriet, and they drove to the Crown in good time, the Randalls' party just sufficiently before them.
>
> Frank Churchill seemed to have been on the watch; and though he did not say much, his eyes declared that he meant to

have a delightful evening. They all walked about together, to see that every thing was as it should be; and within a few minutes were joined by the contents of another carriage, which Emma could not hear the sound of at first, without great surprise. "So unreasonably early!" she was going to exclaim; but she presently found that it was a family of old friends, who were coming, like herself, by particular desire, to help Mr. Weston's judgement; and they were so very closely followed by another carriage of cousins, who had been entreated to come early with the same distinguishing earnestness, on the same errand, that it seemed as if half the company might soon be collected together for the purpose of preparatory inspection.

Emma perceived that her taste was not the only taste on which Mr. Weston depended, and felt, that to be the favourite and intimate of a man who had so many intimates and confidantes, was not the very first distinction in the scale of vanity. She liked his open manners, but a little less of open-heartedness would have made him a higher character.–General benevolence, but not general friendship, made a man what he ought to be.– She could fancy such a man.

The whole party walked about, and looked, and praised again; and then, having nothing else to do, formed a sort of half circle round the fire, to observe in their various modes, till other subjects were started, that, though *May*, a fire in the evening was still very pleasant.

Emma found that it was not Mr. Weston's fault that the number of privy counsellors was not yet larger. They had stopped at Mrs. Bates's door to offer the use of their carriage, but the aunt and niece were to be brought by the Eltons.

Frank was standing by her, but not steadily; there was a restlessness, which showed a mind not at ease. He was looking about, he was going to the door, he was watching for the sound of other carriages,–impatient to begin, or afraid of being always near her.

Mrs. Elton was spoken of. "I think she must be here soon," said he. "I have a great curiosity to see Mrs. Elton, I have heard so much of her. It cannot be long, I think, before she comes."

A carriage was heard. He was on the move immediately; but coming back, said,

"I am forgetting that I am not acquainted with her. I have never seen either Mr. or Mrs. Elton. I have no business to put myself forward."

Mr. and Mrs. Elton appeared; and all the smiles and the

proprieties passed.

"But Miss Bates and Miss Fairfax!" said Mr. Weston, looking about. "We thought you were to bring them."

The mistake had been slight. The carriage was sent for them now. Emma longed to know what Frank's first opinion of Mrs. Elton might be; how he was affected by the studied elegance of her dress, and her smiles of graciousness. He was immediately qualifying himself to form an opinion, by giving her very proper attention, after the introduction had passed.

In a few minutes the carriage returned.–Somebody talked of rain.–"I will see that there are umbrellas, sir," said Frank to his father: "Miss Bates must not be forgotten:" and away he went. Mr. Weston was following; but Mrs. Elton detained him, to gratify him by her opinion of his son; and so briskly did she begin, that the young man himself, though by no means moving slowly, could hardly be out of hearing.

"A very fine young man indeed, Mr. Weston. You know I candidly told you I should form my own opinion; and I am happy to say that I am extremely pleased with him.–You may believe me. I never compliment. I think him a very handsome young man, and his manners are precisely what I like and approve–so truly the gentleman, without the least conceit or puppyism. You must know I have a vast dislike of puppies–quite a horror of them. They were never tolerated at Maple Grove. Neither Mr. Suckling nor me had ever any patience with them; and we used sometimes to say very cutting things! Selina, who is mild almost to a fault, bore with them much better."

While she talked of his son, Mr. Weston's attention was chained; but when she got to Maple Grove, he could recollect that there were ladies just arriving to be attended to, and with happy smiles must hurry away.

5.2 COMMENTARY

The extract forms the first part of an important chapter and a scene that is very characteristic of Jane Austen's method. In the course of the chapter, most of the major characters in the novel are brought together in one place on an occasion that allows for their being disposed in groups and combinations that can be varied from time to time. In the above passage those attending the ball begin to arrive at the crown in groups that are largely determined by their family relationships: first the Westons and Frank Churchill; then, immediately afterwards, Emma and Harriet; then two more carriages of unnamed 'extras' ('a family of old friends' and 'another carriage of cousins'); then, after an interval, the Eltons; and then Miss Bates and Miss Fairfax, whose conveying to the ball (since they do not keep a carriage) has been the subject of a misunderstanding that has dramatic consequences.

Although Jane Austen's narrative method appears to be the conventional, impersonal third-person narrative that is the commonest way of telling a story, a close reading of the extract shows that nearly everything that is communicated is shown as it appears to Emma: what Emma sees and hears is largely what the reader is permitted to 'see' and 'hear', and the judgements and interpretations that are offered are mainly Emma's. However, Jane Austen does provide enough information for the perceptive reader to form his own judgements, which may be at odds with Emma's; although the possibility of an alternative interpretation may not strike the reader on a first reading, a re-reading of the passage in the light of disclosures made later in the book makes it very clear that Emma has failed to see certain important things and has misunderstood others that she has seen.

An early instance of the filtering of the narrative through the heroine's consciousness occurs in line 8, where we are told that for her to meet Frank again at the Crown 'would be better than a common meeting in a crowd'. When we ask: 'Better for whom?' the answer must be, 'Better for Emma'; and though this may appear on a superficial reading to be a statement made by the impersonal narrator, it is actually an expression of Emma's own private thoughts. Again, the statement that Frank 'seemed to have been on the watch' (line 17) reflects Emma's perception of Frank's behaviour and her unspoken reflection upon it. (As a generalisation it may be observed that 'seem', 'appear' and similar words occur frequently in this novel, a clue that what we are given is often 'seemings' rather than actualities - Emma's view of reality rather than reality itself.)

Later in the passage the gap between Emma's perceptions and the truth becomes more significant and more dramatic. Before the Eltons' carriage arrives, Frank is visibly 'not at ease', but no explanation of his excitement is offered since Emma herself, though she is aware of it, does not understand it. Frank professes a curiosity to see Mrs Elton, but this hardly seems sufficient to justify his state of mind; and we may note the cunning ambiguity of the pronouns in lines 53 and 55 ('she' apparently refers to Mrs Elton, but in Frank's mind is much more likely to refer to Jane Fairfax). At this stage Frank pays little attention to Emma - a clue that, whatever his behaviour at other times may suggest, he has no real interest in her.

When the sound of a carriage is heard, Frank's eagerness makes him forget the rules of etiquette, at least momentarily: since he has not yet been introduced to the Eltons, it would be improper for him to rush forward to greet them. Of course his only interest is in Jane, whom he believes to be arriving in their carriage. Jane Austen artfully contrives that Frank shall be disappointed, and his suspense prolonged: there has been a misunderstanding, and Jane has not arrived with the Eltons. When at last the carriage bringing Jane and her aunt does arrive, Frank again dashes forward, this time on the pretext of seeing whether there are umbrellas, and mentioning only Miss Bates.

Throughout this portion of the text, two different versions of reality are in effect presented to the reader: one existing on the surface of the text, the other as a kind of subtext to be provided by the reader on the basis of Jane Austen's hints and clues and subsequent revelations. The surface of the text describes the external behaviour of Frank, as perceived by Emma, with no adequate explanation of why he behaves as he does; the subtext shows the very different Frank who is secretly in love with Jane Fairfax and has a lover's eagerness to see her. The reader is never for a moment allowed to have a glimpse of Frank's unspoken thoughts or inner life, for this would give the game away completely: Jane Austen intends that the reader should share Emma's puzzlement, and that the reader's incomplete understanding of the text he is reading should parallel Emma's imperfect comprehension of the scene she witnesses.

An important element in the situation is Emma's naïveté, and this is also manifested in other ways. For instance, she is surprised to find that Mr Weston has asked a large number of people to arrive early in order to give their opinion of the arrangements at the Crown, whereas she had fondly supposed that he was singling her out for special attention in asking her to do so. She has known Mr Weston for a long time and ought by now, we may consider, to know that this kind of impulsive behaviour is characteristic of him. (We may also reflect that Mr Weston has passed this quality on to his son - another instance of Jane Austen's interest in the way in which the members of a family can share certain traits.) Although Jane Austen as narrator does not make an explicit statement concerning Mr Weston's character as revealed by his behaviour, Emma's reflections upon it are given (lines 31-8), and it is revealing that she should instinctively think of Mr Knightley in this context; even though he is not named and she herself is perhaps hardly aware that she is thinking of him, his character clearly forms a contrast to Mr Weston's in this respect, and he is the obvious example of 'such a man' (line 38). Emma, without quite realising it, is accustomed to thinking of him as a paragon of character and conduct, a yardstick in relation to whom the shortcomings of others can be discerned.

Mrs Elton's character is also developed in this passage, and again the method is not direct statement but a combination of dramatic presentation and the indication of the impression she is making on Emma. Mrs Elton, like some of Shakespeare's fools, unwittingly reveals her shortcomings through her own words and deeds. When she begins to praise Frank before he is out of earshot, the innuendo is that she intends him to hear what she is saying; and there is a strong implication that in the extravagant and rather impertinent praise she showers upon him she intends to flatter his father and to magnify her own self-importance. Her declaration that 'I never compliment' (line 81) is patently untrue, and we may wonder what qualifications she has for deciding whether anyone is or is not a gentleman. Her condescension to Mr Weston, a man older than herself, in assuring him that his son is 'truly the gentleman' is in very doubtful taste; and there is a small but telling sign of her own vulgar background in the error of elementary grammar of which she is guilty ('Neither Mr Suckling nor me': line 86). In the final paragraph of the extract, there is another touch that reveals Mr Weston's character: he is prepared to listen to Mrs Elton's effusions so long as she is praising his son, of whom he is uncritically fond, but finds an excuse to leave her as soon as she moves on to another subject. We cannot imagine Mr Knightley tolerating her ill-bred chatter so patiently. Emma's attitude to Mrs Elton is implied by her wish to know what Frank thinks of her: Emma clearly hopes, and believes, that his verdict on Mrs Elton will be as unfavourable as her own, and there is a hint of malice in the ironic references to 'studied elegance' and 'smiles of graciousness' (lines 67–8). Again, though these phrases appear to be part of the narrative, they are coloured by Emma's own feelings: the sentence beginning 'Emma longed to know. . .' has the effect of giving us an insight into Emma's inner thoughts in the kind of language that she might use in 'speaking' to herself of Mrs Elton.

Ambiguity, which plays such a crucial part in this novel on many levels from incident to dialogue, has already been noted in this passage, especially in connection with Frank Churchill's behaviour and speech. Jane Austen's characteristic irony is also in evidence. The assurance in the opening paragraph that 'every thing was safe' since Frank had kept his promise to come to Highbury for the ball may not be taken at face value by the vigilant reader; and indeed in the course of the chapter we have the time-bomb of Mr Knightley's dancing with Harriet, with its far-reaching consequences, as well as the mystery of Frank Churchill's agitation. 'Safety' is hardly an apt description of the situation of some of the major characters at this point in the story. A lesser example of irony, directed this time at the pettiness of which small-town social life is capable, is found in the stop-gap conversation on the weather (lines 41–3) and the implication that the same banal remarks are made repeatedly by different people ('to observe in their various modes').

Stylistically, the passage illustrates in miniature the considerable range of Jane Austen's verbal effects. The vocabulary ranges from the formal and abstract, as in the weighty Johnsonian reference to 'General benevolence, but not general friendship. . .' (lines 36–7), to the colloquial, notably in the dialogue given to Mrs Elton (e.g. her use of exaggerated phrases such as 'a vast dislike', 'quite a horror', as well as a word such as 'puppy' in the sense of a foolish and impertinent young man). There is a marked contrast between the more formal and literary style of the narrative portions of the text, with such phrases as 'distinguishing earnestness' (line 28) and 'preparatory inspection' (line 30), and the naturalness and realism of the dialogue.

This contrast also operates on the level of syntax. As we would expect, the sentences tend to be longer and more elaborately constructed, with greater use of subordination, in the narrative portions than in the dialogue; the latter, indeed, sometimes makes use (as real speech often does) of the verbless sentence, as in Mr Weston's 'But Miss Bates and Miss Fairfax!' and Mrs Elton's 'A very fine young man indeed, Mr Weston'. But there are also significant and effective contrasts within these two main modes. For instance, Frank's speech in lines 53–5, which is divided into four short sentences, three of them beginning with the same word, suggests his impatience, whereas Mrs Elton's more relaxed state of mind is reflected in her longer and looser sentences (lines 78–88). The narrative style exhibits a similar contrast: it can be crisp and fast-moving, as in the opening paragraph, where 'The day approached, the day arrived. . .' mirrors in its structure the passing of time; but it can also proceed at a much more leisurely pace, as in the last sentence of the third paragraph (lines 22–30).

These varieties of style, between which Jane Austen moves unfussily and unostentatiously, but with the practised ease of a highly skilled writer, correspond to the different functions of her prose, which can narrate action and speech, present unspoken thoughts and reflections and allow authorial irony to play over all. The combination of narrative, dialogue, and what has been termed 'inner speech' to be found in this passage, and in the novel as a whole, represents a remarkable innovation in an early nineteenth-century novel.

6 CRITICAL APPRAISALS

When *Emma* appeared in December 1815, Jane Austen had already published three novels and enjoyed a modest reputation among readers and reviewers. It thus received a reasonable amount of attention from the periodicals of the day. By far the most important of the reviews was that by Sir Walter Scott in the *Quarterly Review*, issued in March 1816. Scott had recently published his own earliest novels, and was to become the most important of Jane Austen's contemporaries in fiction. Although Scott's novels are very different from Jane Austen's, he had the penetration to recognise that she was doing something new and doing it remarkably well. He writes:

> The narrative of all her novels is composed of such common occurrences as may have fallen under the observation of most folks; and her dramatis personae conduct themselves upon the motives and principles which the readers may recognize as ruling their own behaviour and that of most of their acquaintance.

This kind of realism of incident and character, subject-matter and treatment, may strike us as nothing very remarkable, but this is because we are the heirs of a tradition now nearly two centuries old in which Jane Austen was a major influence. Scott saw that, in choosing to write about 'ordinary life' rather than presenting an idealised or sentimentalised version of reality, Jane Austen was helping to create 'the modern novel'. As Brian Southam has said, Scott places her achievement historically, 'as a turning-point in the progress of fiction'.

None of the other contemporary reviewers was anything like as perceptive as Scott in recognising the merits of *Emma* and the significance of what Jane Austen was doing. The *Monthly Review* (July 1816) predicted that 'the work will probably become a favourite with all those who seek for harmless amusement, rather than deep pathos or appalling horrors, in works of fiction', a remark that suggests that the critic was aware that Jane

Austen was attempting something quite different from the novelists of sentiment or of the 'Gothic' school, but failed to appreciate its distinctive excellence. The *British Critic* in the same month described it as 'an amusing, inoffensive and well principled novel', stressed the limited scope of the action ('In few novels is the unity of place preserved. . .the author of *Emma* never goes beyond the boundaries of two private families'), but concluded that 'a very pleasing tale' had been formed out of 's slender materials'. Another woman novelist of the period, Susan Ferrier, wrote in a letter to a friend:

> I have been reading *Emma*, which is excellent, there is no story whatsoever, and the heroine is no better than other people; but the characters are all so true to life, and the style so piquant, that it does not require the adventitious aids of mystery and adventure.

We may feel inclined to disagree with the verdict that 'there is no story whatsoever', but the comment is clearly made – like the rather surprised observation that 'the heroine is no better than other people' – against the background of novelistic fashions that favoured the melodramatic and the highly-coloured.

In the next generation or two, many readers failed to recognise the originality and subtlety of Jane Austen's achievement in *Emma* and made the common mistake of confusing limitation of subject-matter, geography and social range with superficiality and triviality. A cogent reply to such objections has been offered by a modern critic, Arnold Kettle, in his *Introduction to the English Novel* (1951):

> The *smallness* does not matter at all. There is no means of measuring importance by size. What is valuable in a work of art is the depth and truth of the experience it communicates, and such qualities cannot be identified with the breadth of the panorama. We may find out more about life in a railway carriage between Crewe and Manchester than in making a tour round the world. A conversation between two women in the butcher's queue may tell us more about a world war than a volume of despatches from the front.

However, this is not a truth that was clear to many nineteenth-century critics and readers, and we find the frequent appearance of the fallacy of identifying Jane Austen's self-imposed limitations with a crippling lack of significance.

Thus Henry Crabb Robinson noted in his diary on 20 April 1822 that *Emma* was a novel 'evincing great good sense, and an acute observation of human life, but it is not interesting. . .Emma, the heroine, is little more than a clever woman who does foolish things'. John Henry Newman (later Cardinal Newman) wrote in January 1837 that although 'everything

Miss Austen writes is clever. . .there is a want of *body* to the story. The action is frittered away in over-little things'. Charlotte Brontë, who had published *Jane Eyre* three years earlier, wrote in a letter on 12 April 1850 that she had read *Emma* and found a whole dimension of existence lacking in it:

> She does her business of delineating the surface of the lives of genteel English people curiously well. . .she ruffles her reader by nothing vehement, disturbs him by nothing profound: the Passions are perfectly unknown to her; she rejects even a speaking acquaintance with that stormy Sisterhood; even to the Feelings she vouchsafes no more than an occasional graceful but distant recognition; too frequent converse with them would ruffle the smooth elegance of her progress. Her business is not half so much with the human heart as with the human eyes, mouth, hands and feet; what sees keenly, speaks aptly, moves flexibly, it suits her to study, but what throbs fast and full, though hidden, what the blood rushes through, what is the unseen seat of Life and the sentient target of death - *this* Miss Austen ignores. . .

One would never guess from this account that all Jane Austen's novels are love stories, or that *Emma* contains such a scene as that in which the heroine, realising that she loves Mr Knightley, believes him to be in love with another. Though both novels have as their central figure a young woman on the threshold of life, *Jane Eyre* and *Emma* could hardly be more different, representing as they do quite different attitudes to experience and feeling. Charlotte Brontë, committed to a thoroughly Romantic mode of fiction, failed to see that Jane Austen's anti-Romantic novel embodied an equally legitimate enterprise.

Some critics were even harsher in their condemnation of Jane Austen's narrowness of scope and vision (as they deemed it to be). The American writer Emerson found her novels 'vulgar in tone, sterile in invention, imprisoned in the wretched conventions of English society, without genius, wit or knowledge of the world. Never was life so pinched and narrow.' He added that her only subject was 'marriageableness'. Another American, Mark Twain, remarked that reading Jane Austen made him feel 'like a barkeeper entering the Kingdom of Heaven', and in their different ways both these critics were raising objections to the social world she depicts - the middle-class world of the south of England at the beginning of the nineteenth century. They were not prepared to concede that what makes a good or a great novel is not subject but treatment, and that she would not necessarily have been a better novelist if she had chosen to write about, say, the French Revolution.

It is only fair to say that there were other critics at this time ready to pay tribute to Jane Austen's outstanding quality. As early as 1821, Richard Whately, in a long essay in the *Quarterly Review* prompted by the posthumous publication of *Northanger Abbey* and *Persuasion*, made the rather startling point that her dialogue was presented 'with a regard to character hardly exceeded even by Shakespeare himself', and the Shakespearean comparison was later echoed by Lord Macaulay and George Henry Lewes. The latter wrote in *Fraser's Magazine* (December 1847) that 'the greatness of Miss Austen, her marvellous dramatic power, seems more than anything in Scott akin to the greatest quality in Shakespeare', a striking tribute when we recall that Scott's achievement as a novelist was widely respected by the early Victorians.

From about the middle of the century recognition of Jane Austen's greatness becomes more general; there is less stress on her limitations and more on her positive achievement; and *Emma* is sometimes singled out for particular praise. Lewes, writing in *Blackwood's Magazine* in July 1859, found Mrs Elton 'the very best portrait of a vulgar woman we ever saw; she is vulgar in soul, and the vulgarity is indicated by subtle yet unmistakable touches, never by coarse language, or by caricature of any kind' (the praise of Jane Austen's subtlety needs to be seen in relation to the exuberant art of Dickens, the most widely acclaimed novelist of the day). In the following year W. F. Pollock wrote in *Fraser's Magazine* that '*Emma* will generally be recognised by the admirers of Miss Austen as the best of her works. In delicate investigation of the nicer peculiarities of character, and in its perfectly finished execution, it cannot be surpassed'; and again the emphasis - on subtlety of characterisation and artistic skill - is significant in being quite different from that of some earlier critics who had found the novel tame and lacking in interest. A recognition of Jane Austen's insight as a psychologist, and an aesthetic appreciation of the form and technique of her fiction, is beginning to emerge. Mrs Margaret Oliphant, an influential critic and herself a prolific novelist, wrote in *Blackwood's Magazine* in 1870 that *Emma*, 'next to *Pride and Prejudice*, is, in our opinion, her best work' and was 'the work of her mature mind'. Mrs Oliphant adds that 'it is impossible to conceive a more perfect piece of village geography, a scene more absolutely real' than Highbury - a far cry from the criticisms of the physical limitations of Jane Austen's world. As the nineteenth century goes on we hear less of the complaint that Jane Austen is too much caught up with 'the littlenesses and trivialities of life', a phrase that occurs in an unsigned *Westminster Review* articleof 1853 that may be by George Eliot.

By the early twentieth century Jane Austen's reputation is more solidly based and the high place of *Emma* among her novels is widely recognised. The Shakespearean critic A. C. Bradley, for instance, writing in 1911, notes that it is 'the most vivacious of the novels, and with some readers the first favourite'. Bradley adds; 'In its main design it is a comedy, and, as a comedy, unsurpassed, I think, among novels. . .I think the claim may fairly be made for it that, of all [Jane Austen's] novels, it most perfectly executes its design'. A few years later Reginald Farrer, writing in the *Quarterly Review* in July 1917, a century after Scott's famous essay in the same journal, deemed it 'the very climax of Jane Austen's work', adding that 'a real appreciation of *Emma* is the final test of citizenship in her kingdom'. Farrer suggested that 'at every fresh reading you feel anew that you never understood anything like the widening sum of its delights . . . This is *the* novel of character, and of character alone, and of one dominating character in particular'.

Later critics have often endorsed the view that *Emma* is not only Jane Austen's best novel but one of the greatest of English novels. For R. W. Chapman in *Jane Austen: Facts and Problems* (1948) it is 'clearly Jane Austen's masterpiece'. Chapman adds: 'I find the supremacy of *Emma* in the matchless symmetry of its design, in the endless fascination of its technique', and points out that throughout the novel 'we are hardly allowed to see anything except through the heroine's eyes; our vision is actually distorted by her faulty spectacles'. Chapman's emphasis on design and technique, rather than on realism or psychological acumen, indicates a profound shift of emphasis in criticism of the novel in the modern period. The example of Henry James and his imitators, and the influence of critics whose theories are based largely or partly on James's practice, has led *what* is done to seem much less important than *how* it is done; and the reaction against earlier critics whose judgements were based only on a superficial consideration of the content of the novel is complete. In his *The Rhetoric of Fiction* (1961), the American critic Wayne Booth finds at work in *Emma* 'one of the unquestionable masters of the rhetoric of narration'. Booth's persuasive chapter on the novel demonstrates both the skill and the effect of Jane Austen's technique: 'By showing most of the story through Emma's eyes, the author ensures that we shall travel with Emma rather than stand against her'. Another American critic, Lionel Trilling, finds it of all Jane Austen's six novels the 'most fully representative of its author': *Pride and Prejudice* may be more popular, but Emma is 'the greater book - not the more delightful but the greater'. Trilling also judges it 'a very difficult book' and his praise of its protean subtlety and richness is striking:

> The difficulty of *Emma* is never overcome. We never know where to have it. If we finish it at night and think we know what it is up to, we wake the next morning to believe it is up to something quite else. It has become a different book. . .The effect is extraordinary, perhaps unique. The book is like a person - not to be comprehended fully by any other person.

REVISION QUESTIONS

1. Mary Lascelles has said that *Emma* 'presents a deliberately contrived antithesis between the world of actuality and illusion'. Show how Jane Jane Austen presents and dramatises this antithesis in her novel.

2. With close reference to the novel, state what you think R. W. Chapman had in mind when he said '*Emma* is among other things a detective story'.

3. 'Though Emma's faults are comic, they constantly threaten to produce serious harm' (Wayne Booth). Discuss the blend of seriousness and comedy in the novel, and show how Jane Austen contrives to retain a prevailing comic mood.

4. It has been said that the subject of *Emma* is marriage. State your reasons for agreeing or disagreeing with this view.

5. Discuss the comment that while some of the people in the novel are well-developed characters (e.g. Emma, Mr Knightley), others are only caricatures (e.g. Mr Woodhouse, Mrs Elton).

6. Show how Jane Austen exploits social contrasts and social factors in spite of the limited social world that the novel presents.

7. Develop the suggestion that the action of *Emma* is presented in three stages like the acts of a three-act play, and show how this structure accommodates the author's theme.

8. An alternative title for the novel might be *The Education of Emma Woodhouse*. Show in what sense Emma is 'educated' in the course of the story, and how her education comes about.

9. Jane Austen often presents formal or semi-formal social occasions such as a dinner-party or a picnic. With reference to *three* examples of such scenes in *Emma*, discuss the uses to which they are put.

10. W. J. Harvey has said that 'Emma Woodhouse is a heroine who evokes a wide spectrum of critical response, ranging from almost total indulgence and sympathy to almost total hostility and disapproval'. What are your views on the heroine?

11. John Henry Newman complained of *Emma* that 'the action is frittered away in over-little things'. Defend the novel against this charge.

12. In his *Aspects of the Novel*, E. M. Forster says of Jane Austen: 'She is a miniaturist, but never two-dimensional. All her characters are round, or capable of rotundity'. Explain what you consider Forster to mean by 'round' characters, and consider the truth of his statement with reference to *Emma*.

13. '. . . plain, unaffected, gentleman-like English, such as Mr Knightley used even to the woman he was in love with. . .'. Show how Jane Austen uses different varieties of speech to contribute to the creation of her characters.

14. Reviewing *Emma* in 1815, Sir Walter Scott found in it 'the merits of the Flemish school of painting' (i.e. a strong vein of scrupulous domestic realism). Discuss the ways in which this novel presents a convincing picture of life.

FURTHER READING

Frank W. Bradbrook, *Jane Austen: 'Emma'* (London: Edward Arnold, 1961).

J. F. Burrows, *Jane Austen's 'Emma'* (Sydney: Sydney University Press, 1968).

Barbara Hardy, *A Reading of Jane Austen* (London: Peter Owen, 1975).

Arnold Kettle, *An Introduction to the English Novel*, vol I (London: Hutchinson, 1951).

Mary Lascelles, *Jane Austen and her Art* (Oxford: Oxford University Press, 1939).

Marghanita Laski, *Jane Austen and her World* (London: Thames & Hudson, 1969).

David Lodge (ed.), *Jane Austen: 'Emma' - A Casebook* (London: Macmillan, 1968).

Norman Page, *The Language of Jane Austen* (Oxford: Basil Blackwell, 1972).

Stephen M. Parrish (ed.), *Jane Austen: 'Emma'* (New York: Norton, 1972).

K. C. Phillipps, *Jane Austen's English* (London: André Deutsch, 1970).

Brian Southam, *Jane Austen: The Critical Heritage* (London: Routledge & Kegan Paul, 1968).

THE MACMILLAN SHAKESPEARE

General Editor: PETER HOLLINDALE
Advisory Editor: PHILIP BROCKBANK

The Macmillan Shakespeare features:

* clear and uncluttered texts with modernised punctuation and spelling wherever possible;
* full explanatory notes printed on the page facing the relevant text for ease of reference;
* stimulating introductions which concentrate on content, dramatic effect, character and imagery, rather than mere dates and sources.

Above all, The Macmillan Shakespeare treats each play as a work for the theatre which can also be enjoyed on the page.

CORIOLANUS
Editor: Tony Parr

THE WINTER'S TALE
Editor: Christopher Parry

MUCH ADO ABOUT NOTHING
Editor: Jan McKeith

RICHARD II
Editor: Richard Adams

HENRY IV, PART I
Editor: Peter Hollindale

HENRY IV, PART II
Editor: Tony Parr

HENRY V
Editor: Brian Phythian

AS YOU LIKE IT
Editor: Peter Hollindale

A MIDSUMMER NIGHT'S DREAM
Editor: Norman Sanders

THE MERCHANT OF VENICE
Editor: Christopher Parry

THE TAMING OF THE SHREW
Editor: Robin Hood

TWELFTH NIGHT
Editor: E. A. J. Honingmann

THE TEMPEST
Editor: A. C. Spearing

ROMEO AND JULIET
Editor: James Gibson

JULIUS CAESAR
Editor: D. R. Elloway

MACBETH
Editor: D. R. Elloway

HAMLET
Editor: Nigel Alexander

ANTONY AND CLEOPATRA
Editors: Jan McKeith and Richard Adams

OTHELLO
Editors: Celia Hilton and R. T. Jones

KING LEAR
Editor: Philip Edwards

MILTON: COMUS AND SAMSON AGONISTES
Julian Lovelock

MILTON: PARADISE LOST
A. E. Dyson and Julian Lovelock

POETRY OF THE FIRST WORLD WAR
Dominic Hibberd

ALEXANDER POPE: THE RAPE OF THE LOCK
John Dixon Hunt

SHELLEY: SHORTER POEMS & LYRICS
Patrick Swinden

SPENSER: THE FAERIE QUEEN
Peter Bayley

TENNYSON: IN MEMORIAM
John Dixon Hunt

THIRTIES POETS: 'THE AUDEN GROUP'
Ronald Carter

WORDSWORTH: LYRICAL BALLADS
A. R. Jones and W. Tydeman

WORDSWORTH: THE PRELUDE
W. J. Harvey and R. Gravil

W. B. YEATS: POEMS 1919–1935
E. Cullingford

W. B. YEATS: LAST POEMS
Jon Stallworthy

THE NOVEL AND PROSE

JANE AUSTEN: EMMA
David Lodge

JANE AUSTEN: NORTHANGER ABBEY AND PERSUASION
B. C. Southam

JANE AUSTEN: SENSE AND SENSIBILITY, PRIDE AND PREJUDICE AND MANSFIELD PARK
B. C. Southam

CHARLOTTE BRONTË: JANE EYRE AND VILLETTE
Miriam Allott

EMILY BRONTË: WUTHERING HEIGHTS
Miriam Allott

BUNYAN: THE PILGRIM'S PROGRESS
R. Sharrock

CONRAD: HEART OF DARKNESS, NOSTROMO AND UNDER WESTERN EYES
C. B. Cox

CONRAD: THE SECRET AGENT
Ian Watt

CHARLES DICKENS: BLEAK HOUSE
A. E. Dyson

CHARLES DICKENS: HARD TIMES, GREAT EXPECTATIONS AND OUR MUTUAL FRIEND
N. Page

GEORGE ELIOT: MIDDLEMARCH
Patrick Swinden

GEORGE ELIOT: THE MILL ON THE FLOSS AND SILAS MARNER
R. P. Draper

HENRY FIELDING: TOM JONES
Neil Compton

E. M. FORSTER: A PASSAGE TO INDIA
Malcolm Bradbury

HARDY: THE TRAGIC NOVELS
R. P. Draper

HENRY JAMES: WASHINGTON SQUARE AND THE PORTRAIT OF A LADY
Alan Shelston

JAMES JOYCE: DUBLINERS AND A PORTRAIT OF THE ARTIST AS A YOUNG MAN
Morris Beja

D. H. LAWRENCE: THE RAINBOW AND WOMEN IN LOVE
Colin Clarke

D. H. LAWRENCE: SONS AND LOVERS
Gamini Salgado

SWIFT: GULLIVER'S TRAVELS
Richard Gravil

THACKERAY: VANITY FAIR
Arthur Pollard

TROLLOPE: THE BARSETSHIRE NOVELS
T. Bareham

VIRGINIA WOOLF: TO THE LIGHTHOUSE
Morris Beja

DRAMA

CONGREVE: COMEDIES
Patrick Lyons

T. S. ELIOT: PLAYS
Arnold P. Hinchliffe

JONSON: EVERY MAN IN HIS HUMOUR AND THE ALCHEMIST
R. V. Holdsworth

JONSON: VOLPONE
J. A. Barish

MARLOWE: DR. FAUSTUS
John Jump

MARLOWE: TAMBURLAINE, EDWARD II AND THE JEW OF MALTA
John Russell Brown

MEDIEVAL ENGLISH DRAMA
Peter Happé

O'CASEY: JUNO AND THE PAYCOCK, THE PLOUGH AND THE STARS AND THE SHADOW OF A GUNMAN
R. Ayling

JOHN OSBORNE: LOOK BACK IN ANGER
John Russell Taylor

WEBSTER: THE WHITE DEVIL AND THE DUCHESS OF MALFI
R. V. Holdsworth

WILDE: COMEDIES
W. Tydeman

SHAKESPEARE

SHAKESPEARE: ANTONY AND CLEOPATRA
John Russell Brown

SHAKESPEARE: CORIOLANUS
B. A. Brockman

SHAKESPEARE: HAMLET
John Jump

SHAKESPEARE: HENRY IV PARTS I AND II
G. K. Hunter

SHAKESPEARE: HENRY V
Michael Quinn

SHAKESPEARE: JULIUS CAESAR
Peter Ure

SHAKESPEARE: KING LEAR
Frank Kermode

SHAKESPEARE: MACBETH
John Wain

SHAKESPEARE: MEASURE FOR MEASURE
G. K. Stead

SHAKESPEARE: THE MERCHANT OF VENICE
John Wilders

SHAKESPEARE: A MIDSUMMER NIGHT'S DREAM
A. W. Price

SHAKESPEARE: MUCH ADO ABOUT NOTHING AND AS YOU LIKE IT
John Russell Brown

SHAKESPEARE: OTHELLO
John Wain

SHAKESPEARE: RICHARD II
N. Brooke

SHAKESPEARE: THE SONNETS
Peter Jones

SHAKESPEARE: THE TEMPEST
D. J. Palmer

SHAKESPEARE: TROILUS AND CRESSIDA
Priscilla Martin

SHAKESPEARE: TWELFTH NIGHT
D. J. Palmer

SHAKESPEARE: THE WINTER'S TALE
Kenneth Muir